No Strings

In Search of Dickie Jones

By Ann Snuggs

Albany, Georgia

No Strings: In Search of Dickie Jones
Copyright © 2016 Ann Snuggs. All Rights Reserved.

No part of this book may be reproduced in any form or by any means, electronic, mechanical, digital, photocopying or recording, except for the inclusion in a review, without permission in writing from the the publisher.

Published in the USA by
BearManor Media
P.O. Box 71426
Albany, GA 31708
www.BearManorMedia.com

Softcover Edition
ISBN-10: 1593939701
ISBN-13: 978-1-59393-970-0

Cover design by Ann Snuggs

Printed in the United States of America

Table of Contents

Acknowledgements — ix
Foreword — xi
Introduction — xiii

Or So I Was Told — 1
Hello, Hollywood — 5
Cliffhanging — 15
Hail, Hail, the Gang's All Here — 31
Go West, Young Man — 37
It's All a Blank — 73
I Remember ... — 83
Mr. Stewart — 91
"Little Wooden Head" — 97
The Early 1940s — 105
On the Air — 113
Returning to Film — 119
On the Rock — 123
Cool, Man, Cool — 131
Old Gunslingers — 137
Jones & Jones — 141
Did You Know ...? — 147
Tying It Up — 163

Annotated Filmography — 167
Sources — 189

Appendix I: Categorizing the Early Films — 191
Appendix II: Billed Together — 195
Appendix III: Questionable Credits — 205

Index of Film Titles — 209
Index — 213

Once again, for Betty and Dick

Acknowledgements

The importance of Betty Jones to this development of this book cannot be overestimated. Her determination to have at least a part of Dick's years in film told was unrelenting. I caught something of her persistence, and only by the hardest did we finally get Dick to share some of his memories. He was one of the most private persons I have ever known, and only by agreeing to stay away from areas he did not wish to share was I able to get him to talk. Thank you, Betty and Dick.

From the start, in my published writing Kristofer Todd Upjohn has supported me—reading, editing, suggesting, and commenting. His backing has been invaluable. I wouldn't want to do it without him.

Deep appreciation to Sue Winsor, who also read parts and made suggestions.

Also to the many friends who gave me encouragement as I struggled through this process, Frances, Donna, and Becky, especially.

Thanks to Dwight Morrow, who helped in the search for hard-to-find films Dick was in and often was the one who found them. His help was a blessing.

Thanks to my friend Frances Taylor for the great picture of L.Q. Jones used with the Foreword.

Thanks to Boyd and Donna Magers, who supported the idea of this book even before Dick agreed to talk and make it a reality.

A very, very special thank you to the delightful L.Q. Jones, who shared his memories of working with Dick and reluctantly agreed to write the foreword for this book. It was a joy to work and visit with him on this. He was the perfect person to write the opening words because he, like I, knew Dick Jones as a man with no strings, his own man.

Foreword

Dickie Jones was
                      trustworthy
                 loyal
                    helpful
                       friendly
                          courteous
                             kind
                                obedient
                                   cheerful
                                     thrifty
                                        brave
                                           clean
                                               reverent.*

He was also my friend.

As you read more about him, he will be yours too.

                                                      * Boy Scouts of America

Photo by Frances Taylor

Introduction

WHEN DICK JONES DIED, his obituary in *The New York Times* called him, "...an actor whose face should be more familiar than it is...." That's accurate. Dick appeared in nearly 100 movies and more than 200 television productions. He performed in motion pictures and television, as well as radio. But the general public – especially the *younger* general public – knows his voice, not his face, for his is the voice of Disney's Pinocchio.

Children of the 1950s know his face as Buffalo Bill, Jr., a Saturday morning television hero, or those a little older remember him as Dick West, saddle pal to the Range Rider, but those appearances built on years of experience in front of a camera.

When I told people this book about Dick's film work would be called *No*

Strings: In Search of Dickie Jones, they immediately remarked, "Oh, because he was the voice of Pinocchio." That's not the reason, although it does give a tip of the hat to the role.

Young Dickie Jones' career was controlled by his mother. She was adamant about not contracting him to one studio. His first long-term contract of that kind came about when he was an adult, after World War II. Young Dickie had no strings on his talent, and throughout his life, Dick Jones was his own man. No strings on him.

The downside of the failure of his mother to tie him down was that he lacked studio backing, which might have promoted his multiple talents into a blockbuster career of the magnitude of Shirley Temple, Mickey Rooney, or other child stars of the 1930s. For Dick Jones was as versatile as they came. He danced; he sang—though not his favorite action; he was doing stunts from his first film; he cried on demand; he was a quick study at learning lines and following direction; and he was a terrific actor—as natural-looking, natural-sounding, and as convincing as any child on screen in his time. Sometimes, he was the best actor in the film.

Nevertheless, in order to see the young Dickie in action it is necessary to search. A number of the films I tried to locate to watch his work seem to have been lost forever for viewing by the general public. In some films, he was uncredited. In many films of that day, only a handful of the actors were in the credits, so those listed past sixth or seventh didn't exist. In a situation of confusion that aggravated both, he and Dickie Moore were constantly confused when researchers went back to make credit lists. The researchers either did not actually watch the films or didn't recognize which Dickie was before their eyes—and the boys did *not* look alike.

An example of this is *The Pecos Kid*. It's an entertaining film, firmly rooted in its B-era, with Fred Kohler, Jr. in the title role. "Dickie Jones" is listed as "Donald Pecos as a boy" but that's Dickie Moore on the screen as plain as day. The reverse also may be seen in the difficult to find film, *Fifteen Wives*. Dickie Moore is credited, but I have a still of Dick Jones from the film.

All the challenges in putting together an accurate list of Dick's appearances and locating copies of the films generated the subtitle, *In Search of Dickie Jones*. Dick's inclination toward privacy also encouraged that, as even after Dick agreed to talk about his career, it was like pulling teeth to get him to elaborate on some topics.

My connection with Dick began with an admiration for a television hero in my childhood, one I was blessed to meet as an adult and who became a friend for life.

We met at the 1987 Memphis Film Festival and hit it off immediately. In his down time there, Dick joined me and my friends to visit over coffee and even over a hand of cards.

Dick Jones concentrates on a hand of gin rummy.

Through the years, Dick and his wife, Betty, and I would meet at festivals and events. At an event in Tombstone, Arizona, Betty suggested that I write about Dick's film career or guide his memoirs. I was thrilled. Dick was not. The convention at Tombstone gave us a chance to talk and visit but Dick refused a commitment to the project.

Dick Jones (right) and the author (second from left) visit with Harry Carey, Jr. and his wife, Marilyn Fix Carey at a breakfast event at Tombstone.

For years, every time we got together, and sometimes in phone conversations, Betty and I worked at tearing down Dick's resistance to sharing his memories. One day, he said to me, "I don't want to dig up bones."

That gave me the clue to the way to get him talking. I replied, "Dick, you don't have to dig up bones. Just tell me what you want to tell. You *cannot* answer questions if you don't want to talk about that subject." That opened his mind and mouth to starting work on this project.

It has been slow going, with some major setbacks even before his sudden death, but after searching, talking, and learning how tremendously talented Dick Jones was as the screen minutes rolled before my eyes, I have found something of who Dick Jones really was—multitalented, multifaceted, capable of many things on many levels, and modest and unassuming through it all. Through this book, I hope to honor this very special man by sharing with his fans what I have learned.

Or So I Was Told

On the twenty-fifth day of February 1927 in Synder, Texas, Richard P. Jones made his first public appearance. Unlike babies of today, his birth was not recorded on video. No smartphone pictures were immediately zapped out to extended family and friends. Though the audience that day may have been small, it would not be long before the young boy from Texas would be entertaining the world.

Between that day and the day Hoot Gibson saw him performing and said the fateful words that would send him to California and a career as a child actor, the family moved to McKinney, Texas. The circumstances surrounding that move were never recorded, and Dick was far too young to remember. By the time Dick was four, the family was in McKinney, Texas, and he had his own act. He was "The World's Youngest Trick Rider and Trick Roper," a big title for a small boy.

Let's hear about those early years in his own words.

Just like most people, my memories from my youngest years are hazy. A lot of what I "remember" is actually what I was told by others.

Somebody told me I started walking and riding about the same time. I don't remember when I didn't ride and rope. I don't remember learning how to do it. I don't know how it came about, where it came up. Some of the horse stuff I think I got by trying to emulate Tom Mix. He fascinated me with some of the stuff he did.

I don't remember the first time I performed as "The World's Youngest Trick Rider and Trick Roper." All I know is what my aunt or my mother told me and they didn't tell me much about it.

The closest thing I know . . . is I've got a picture of me doing a "Ta-da!" Tipping my hat, holding this spotted horse's reins.

(Unfortunately, this picture seems to have been lost in the shuffle. When Dick tried to locate it to be included with his stories, he did not find it among his memorabilia.)

I don't know where this horse was kept. My aunt said this picture was taken in back of our house in McKinney, Texas. I could spin a rope. I could do a butterfly, Texas skip. Yeah, I was a trick roper.

Dick described his routine:

I'd stand up in the saddle with the horse running—girls call it a hippodrome—where they lean over the brow band of the horse with their feet under the hoop. I would do an under the neck from the saddle horn and back up to the saddle again, and then I'd do a fender drag like the Russian Cossacks would. I'd only do maybe two or three tricks twice because two or three times around the arena was all they'd let you do.

As with all early memories, Dick's were patchy and incomplete. When pressed, he recalled some bits and pieces.

There are a couple of things that flash back in my mind about living there, but I can't put a whole story to them. Like the time I brought a miniature horse into the kitchen. I have memories of what I think was the only time my dad spanked me because I brought this miniature horse into the house. It was smaller than a Shetland pony, but it was a horse. That was in the early days of miniature horses.

I brought it into the house and my dad boosted my butt for doing it. He said, "That horse is not to be in this house."

I don't know where I would have a horse or keep a horse. It seems to me that there was a barn behind our house but I don't know why we would have a barn in the city. I asked my aunt these questions—she was the only one who could tell me—and she said, "I don't have the foggiest because I didn't pay any attention to you. You were just a brat." So, I never got any information out of her.

I just have glimpses of the stuff like that.

I got bucked off a calf, trying to ride it in the back yard, and I got tangled up in the milk cow's tether—I don't know how—but it chewed my leg up pretty bad. It damn near broke my leg. The cow started bucking and I got tangled up in the chain. I don't know how I got out of it but I didn't break my leg.

I remember getting on the milk wagon with the guy who delivered milk—horse-drawn wagon—and they were mad at me so I went downtown and hid in the drugstore behind the soda fountain.

I remember getting a jar and filling it up with lightning bugs to make me a lantern.

Besides getting into little boy mischief, Dick performed. He would gain his first radio experience, though it was music rather than the scripted material he would later do. He shared some sketchy remembrances:

My mother would drive me into Dallas where I'd work on the Cowboy Ramblers Radio Show. *I was called the Little Cowboy Rambler, and I'd play the ukulele and sing on radio.*

I was half cowboy in a fancy satin shirt and had a pair of English puttees [jodhpurs] in Texas. When I came out to California and started wandering around moving pictures, I started accumulating cowboy stuff.

Edmund Richard "Hoot" Gibson was one of the "Big Five" cowboy heroes of silent film. He not only rode across the silver screen in movies but also went on the road for Wild West shows and at rodeos and extravaganzas. It was his words that propelled little Dickie Jones into the world of film.

"The World's Youngest Trick Rider and Trick Roper" was performing in Dallas where Gibson was the star attraction.

Dick describes the minutes that changed his life from that of a Texas boy who would grow up Texan to a child star on the big screen in Hollywood.

We lived in McKinney when I did the Dallas Centennial Rodeo, where Hoot Gibson saw me. When I performed there, I was on a big dark-colored horse, probably a bay or a black. There's no way I could touch the ground, but I did tricks from the saddle and ended up doing a fender drag on the inside on the left hand side of the horse, going around the arena counterclockwise. When I'd come back around, I'd come up on the top of the saddle and stand up and tip my hat and, "Ta-da!"

Hoot Gibson saw that and told my mother, "That kid ought to be in movies." My mother said, "Whoopee!" and away we went to Hollywood.

Things didn't quite happen that quickly, although Betty Jones assured me Dick's mother started packing that night. However, within a couple of weeks, "The World's Youngest Trick Rider and Trick Roper," his mother, and Hoot Gibson's manager were on a train bound for California and fame.

Their destination was the ranch at Saugus, California, in which Hoot had bought a third interest in 1930.

Dick remembered:

I stayed out at Hoot Gibson's ranch at Saugus about two years. He had his rodeo stock there and that famous bucking horse, Tumbleweed. I used to ride him around like he was a Shetland pony. Put him in the bucking shoot and nobody could ride him. I was five or six years old.

When we got to California, Hoot was on the road all of the time. I think he took me around and introduced my mother to the agents and casting directors and it went from there. I never worked with him.

That's one of the ironies of Dick's participation in so many Westerns. He worked with most of the major Western stars of the heyday of Western films with the exception of the one who brought him to California and opened the door to his screen career, Hoot Gibson, but he does have a lasting memory.

One thing I remember about Hoot Gibson was that he always started out with, "Say . . . ." I always remember that about him.

Hello, Hollywood

WHILE HIS MOTHER WAS SEEKING CONNECTIONS to turn her son into a star, Dick was learning skills that would make him more marketable.

One of those was dance, a talent in which he excelled because of his natural athletic abilities.

I didn't tap dance in Texas. Dancing was part of my training to be an actor. I remember going to a place on the upper floor of Bryan's Furniture Moving Co. It was about a nine- or ten-story thing. It was the Bud Murray School of Dance.

We started off with a time step, I guess, and ended up doing whole routines and choreographing shows. I did a couple of Shirley Temple pictures as one of the dancers. I did all kinds of that stuff in Our Gang comedies. Bud Murray's school did the dances in Our Gang.

I stopped dancing when they said I had to take ballet and had to wear tights and a tutu. That was the end of that.

However, little Dickie's first performance wasn't tapping on the boards but flying through the air strapped into a harness. It was tough to recognize that bright little face, and not just because of his rapid movement.

Al Jolson was the star of *Wonder Bar,* and the production number, "Goin' to Heaven on a Mule," would become controversial, for Jolson and all involved, including flying cherub Dickie, were in blackface.

"Goin' to Heaven on a Mule" wasn't the only scene that raised eyebrows. The show barely made it into theaters because of risqué elements that pushed the limits of the Production Code. A man dancing with another man in a nightclub coupled with Jolson's flip comment about it almost prevented the film's release.

Wonder Bar is a strange and interesting movie. Set in Paris, under "genre," it is defined at Internet Movie Database as "crime, drama, musical, romance." That's quite a combo, and it *is* every one of those. With Busby Berkeley production numbers and lavish costumes highlighting the film, it is fascinating though severely dated. The Vaudeville exchange vignettes, such as the one between Jolson and the Russian count, are anomalous in this century and a bit jarring. However, the plot is twisted and timeless. It is the trappings that date this so dreadfully. The basic action could fly today.

Dickie's aerial stunt appearance is only in the finale. Courtesy of the freeze frame capabilities of newer tech players, it is now possible to stop the action enough to find those cherub cheeks under the blackface.

All the controversy surrounding *Wonder Bar* was irrelevant to a child. Dick's memories of the film are sketchy.

My first job was an aerial stunt in Wonder Bar *with Al Jolson but you wouldn't know me because I was dressed up like a child angel with a white robe and a pair of wings and black face. I had an aerial harness on and I flew all over Stage 13 at Warner Bros. I was thirty feet above Al Jolson. When I saw him, I was swinging over him in the production number of "Goin' to Heaven on a Mule." I remember that I did it and that's all. I was only four years old or something like that. They'd get me up there and wouldn't let me down.*

That was my first job. Then I progressed to working with a group of kids in other pictures.

Dick had no significant interaction with Jolson, nor with the other stars of the production, Dick Powell, Kay Francis, Dolores Del Rio, or actors in lesser roles, such as Robert Barrat, with whom he would work later in several films including *The Adventures of Mark Twain*.

That little angel face was easier to spot in *Babes in Toyland*, aka *March of the Wooden Soldiers*, with Stan Laurel and Oliver Hardy. Laurel and Hardy's version of the story of the childhood characters came from Hal Roach. Dick was not the only child who worked in *Our Gang* comedies to appear in it but it predates his *Our Gang* shorts.

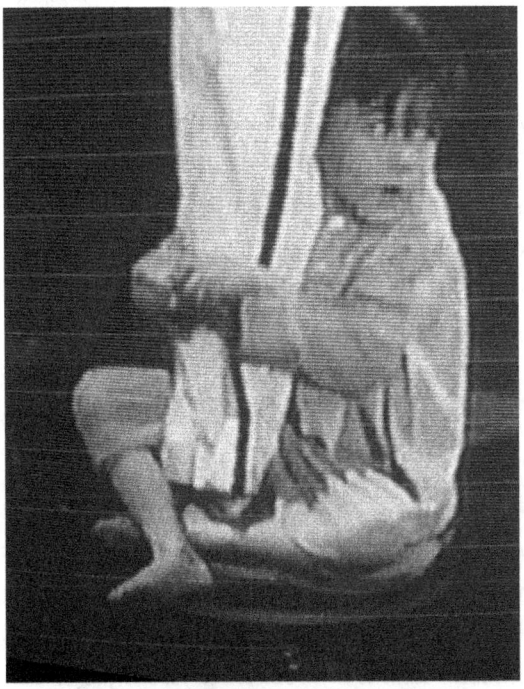

A fuzzy but recognizable screenshot from my television of little Dickie clinging to the soldier's leg.

Though he, along with the other children, ran through several scenes, the only place his face is plain is in the climax when the wooden soldiers march to triumph over the bogeymen who have overrun Toyland. Dick can be seen clinging to the foot of one of the wooden soldiers, and that action is his stand-out memory from the picture.

The thing I remember most about Babes in Toyland *was that they could never find me when it was time to work. I was too busy playing on the back lot on the sailboats on another set. I never liked the set I was working on. I always wanted to wander off and look at another one. I was always getting lost and missing out on a lot of the shots.*

In the production number, when Bo-Peep loses her sheep, I remember the crowd. We just followed along when the director said, "You move over here and you move over there."

I remember riding on the pedestal feet of the wooden soldiers and crashing through the wall on the wooden soldier's foot. It was fun riding around on that wooden soldier.

I was only about six when it was made.

One of Dick's memories about the Laurel and Hardy film was an uncredited assistant director on the picture whom he remembered as a top man to work with children, Gordon Douglas. Douglas would also be at the helm of a number of *Our Gang* comedies, including *The Pigskin Palooka*, one of Dick's *Our Gang* appearances.

There's a talent to directing kids. Nobody goes on set directing kids other than the director. If a director is working with kids, he either does it himself or gets an assistant who can handle kids.

You get down on your knees and look them in the eyeball. Then you tell them a story or how they are supposed to react to that story and tell them when you say action they are supposed to act out that story.

You're talking with four- and five-year-olds. At that age, they can't read the script, so you tell them what to say. You get six-, seven-, eight-year-olds, they can read it in advance.

When I couldn't read, I was told what to say and to do. After I could read, I'd get a script and I'd mark my script up. The director would tell me what he wanted, and I'd go from there.

It takes a special person to direct kids like that, and Gordon Douglas was perfection. And John English. Gordon Douglas and John English were great at doing action Western serials and Our Gang comedies.

Dick proved to be in demand during his debut year in films, with appearances in nine pictures that were released in 1934. Most of them were scenes that he did and promptly deleted from his memory, but a few left some distinct memories.

In *Now and Forever*, Jerry and Toni Day (Gary Cooper and Carole Lombard) flit around the world living on cons and "chasing trains," as Toni says, until Jerry retrieves his daughter Penny (Shirley Temple) to live with them. Penny catches the eye and heart of an elderly, extremely wealthy lady, Mrs. Crane (Charlotte Granville), who wants to take Penny and give her all the advantages. Mrs. Crane gives little Penny a party.

Dick is one of the children at the party. Penny performs for her guests and becomes restless with the situation.

Henry Hathaway directed the film. Even though he had no lines, Dick managed to make an impression on the director.

Henry Hathaway sure didn't like me at all. I was working with a bunch of kids on a Shirley Temple picture. I was up in the front row and I was fidgety. It upset him and he yelled, "Stop! Cut! Hold it! Get that kid with the ants in his pants in the back." That kid was me.

Dick made two early films with "Wives" in the title, *Fifteen Wives* and *Strange Wives*. Neither made a deep impression on Dick and few other people seem to recall them either, as an extensive search for available prints to view at home turned up nothing. They did exist and Dick had the stills to prove it.

He had no still from another "missing" picture in that first year, *The Life of Vergie Winters*. The plotline and stars can be found in film history sources, but video copies of it are not on the market. It starred Ann Harding and John Boles. Dick's role is not credited.

Conway Tearle and Natalie Moorhead confront each other as Dick Jones and an unidentified player look on in *Fifteen Wives*.

Dick Jones and Buster Phelps are reprimanded in this scene from *Strange Wives*. Dick commented, "I have little recall of *Strange Wives*. I played a twin. I've still got a still of it."

First young Dickie appeared with Jolson, then later that year he appeared in a film with another entertainer who graced the Vaudeville stage, Eddie Cantor. *Kid Millions* is not generally considered one of the best of the Cantor musicals and is filled with extremely dated humor left over from Vaudeville. It was likely more charming to audiences of the 1930s than filmgoers of today.

However, the color production number finale is well-worth checking out. Dick is one of the horde of child performers that fills this spectacular color-tinted footage. It was sensational in its day and remains impressive after all the years.

If, and only IF, the viewer knows where and when to look (watch for the red tie in the film), Dick can be recognized among the children crowding the window of the ice cream factory. "Dickie" written on the picture marks him in this still. Spotting him in the actual dance sequence is much more difficult.

What I remember about Kid Millions *is the scene where we were supposed to be in the candy shop and have a soda. I forget what song Eddie Cantor was singing. There were giant sodas about ten feet tall and they put us on hydraulic seats like at a soda shop and they'd run us up the top and we'd act like we were putting a big straw in our mouths and we'd suck on that and then we'd go down in the ice cream soda – down in the glass. It was a specialized dance routine.*

Dick appeared in his first serial shortly after beginning film work. One of the directors of that cliffhanger was Armand Schaefer, with whom Dick would work again farther along in his career. Whether or not Schaefer remembered the professionalism of young Dickie at that early age and favored him for later roles is unknown.

Burn 'Em Up Barnes was a typical early-1930s serial. The plot was standard with the hero trying to save the rather ditzy female. In this one, Burn 'Em Up Barnes (Jack Mulhall) gives up car racing after the death of a close friend and vows to take care of his friend's younger brother Bobbie (Frankie Darro). He goes into partnership with Marjorie Temple (Lola Lane) in a transportation business. She doesn't know her land is loaded with oil but the villains do and will stop at nothing to get her land. It's up to Burn 'Em Up to save her and the business.

A group of children say goodbye to Burn 'Em Up Barnes (Jack Mulhall) as they leave the bus. Dick's cap is marked with his name.

Barnes and his partner contract to transport schoolchildren with their buses. Dick is one of the children dropped off at school in the first chapter before all the cliffhanging action sequences take over. He has several lines with Jack Mulhall (Burn 'Em Up) before he enters the school building. He has more lines in Chapter Seven but the job left little impression on him.

What I remember about that one is working with Frankie Darro. I was always a fan of his and the way he could tumble.

Darro's acrobatic skills are as impressive to the viewers of this serial as they were to Dick, who worked on several movies with Frankie and mentioned his tumbling skills whenever Darro's name came up. Another of those was made the same year as *Burn 'Em Up Barnes*, *Little Men*.

The perennially popular Louisa May Alcott novel, *Little Women*, was a noted movie in 1933. A version of the novel's sequel, *Little Men*, was made in 1934. Dick had the role of Dolly, one of the younger boys at the school run by Jo (Erin O'Brien-Moore) and Professor Bhaer (Ralph Morgan), though the character names in the film did not exactly match the characters in the book. Darro played Dan.

I had a good part in Little Men. *I was all the way through the darn thing. That was the one with Erin O'Brien-Moore, Ralph Morgan, and Frankie Darro. I was amazed at Frankie Darro's athletic ability. He did a tumbling routine in that. He could do a round-off.*

Dickie Moore and I were friends then. Then it got so that he was called "Dickie Jones" and I was called "Dickie Moore" and we both got upset about that.

A while back, someone came out with a flier—they had a get-together, sort of like a party thrown by one of our good friends outside of the business but who invites a lot of old cowboy movie stars. They were circulating a color print—like a lobby card—with Little Men. *All around the edges were pictures of the different persons who were in it. It was in color. It brought back my memories of Frankie Darro and his tumbling. I worked with Frankie Darro in '34, '35; then worked with him again in '40 because he was Lampwick, the deadbeat, dead end kid in Pinocchio. Then I worked with him in a couple of Gene Autry movies. He was a nice guy. I liked him. He sure could tumble.*

Cliffhanging

A COUPLE OF SERIALS began Dick's second year in the movie business. He appeared in *Queen of the Jungle*, in which he played David Worth, Jr. "as a boy," and *Call of the Savage*, in the role of Jan Trevor "as a boy."

These roles would kick off almost a decade of roles in which the young Dickie would "grow up" into a number of adult actors, including the likes of Cary Grant, John Payne, and Fredric March.

In *Queen of the Jungle*, a 1935 serial with Mary Kornman and Reed Howes, Dick plays the child David Worth and gets fourth billing. Though he only appears in Chapter One, his credit runs at the first of every chapter. He deserved it. Even at his young age, his performance is totally natural and he has his lines down pat. He "out-acts" many of the older cast.

The serial is standard, low-budget early fare. Lots of stock footage, especially of the wild animals. The white men search for radium in the Garden of Rad. The Sacred Cult of Mu guards the valley and the radium deposits. Dick's father and the father of his young playmate Joan Lawrence (Marilyn Spinner) are the force behind the search.

Dave and Joan are playing hide-and-seek when Joan decides to hide in the new hot air balloon. The adults come to find the children and separate to search when Dave tells them, "We were playing hide-and-go-seek and I can't find her." A lion (stock footage) charges Dave's father and the man with him, and to escape the lion, they loose the balloon and grab the attached rope ladder. The ladder breaks and both men are killed when they drop to the ground.

Young David Worth (Dick Jones) clings to the hand of Mary Lawrence (Mary Kornman) as he sees his father fall to his death.

Dick demonstrates his ability to cry on cue when he runs to the body of his father. Joan floats away and is shot down with a flaming arrow by a member of the tribe honoring the "Great God Rad." The natives are not sure what to make of Joan but decide to let Rad save her or let her be killed.

The early footage of Chapter Two shows how Joan survives to become the Queen of the Jungle (Mary Kornman). Then twenty years pass. Dick has grown up to be the adult David Worth (Reed Howes), still searching for Joan.

Dick commented:

Queen of the Jungle. *Mary Kornman. I was in the very first chapter as somebody as a child and I got billing. So I got billing on all of the chapters as they keep on going even though I was only in one.*

Lafe McKee, who would shortly work with Dick in *Trail of the Hawk*, is the villain Kali. Their screen time did not cross in this serial.

In his second jungle serial of 1935, *Call of the Savage*, Dickie grows up to be Noah Beery, Jr. The white men go into the jungle this time to find a cure for infantile paralysis (polio). Dr. Harry Trevor asks to take his wife and son Jan (Dick, in Chapter One) with him. In the depths of the jungle, Jan's only playmate is the chimp, Chicma.

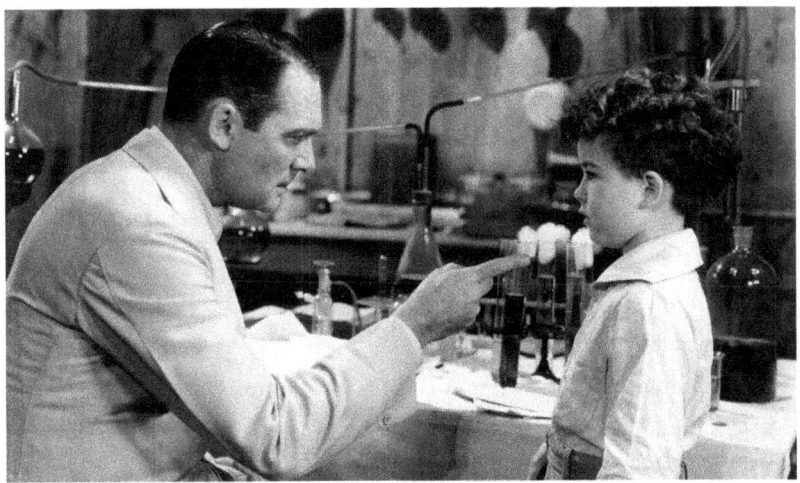

Dr. Frank Bracken (Walter Miller) lays down the law to young Jan Trevor (Dick Jones) about being in the lab.

The search for the cure is a competition among four doctors. Of course, Jan's father and one doctor are good and the other two are in it for the prize money. Jan's father discovers the formula first. To protect it he engraves half of it on a wristband which he puts on Jan's wrist.

Before the villains can take it from the boy and steal the half in the lab, the jungle cats—no explanation is given why so many cages of them sit around the camp—break loose and attack Jan's parents. A huge explosion destroys the lab. Jan's mother is killed and his father loses his mind. In the confusion, Jan wanders away through the jungle with Chicma.

A close-up on the bracelet on Dick's wrist fades into the wristband on the wrist of Noah Beery, Jr., swinging through the jungle. Dick didn't even complete the Chapter One before "growing up." Though he is farther down in the credits, his credit is included on every chapter.

Mu must have been popular in jungle films of the era. They are hunting for the lost Kingdom of Mu in this one, too.

Dick had to have some cosmetic alterations for this job.

I had to have my hair curled and I couldn't figure out why. Then, I remembered I grew up to be Noah Beery, Jr. and his hair was curly. I got billing all the way through the whole thing. I was billed in all the chapters of that, too.

The Adventures of Frank Merriwell was another Chapter One only appearance for Dick, who is uncredited in this serial. However, his easily recognizable face is behind Jean Rogers, who plays Frank's girl Elsie Belwood, in the titles that run at the first of every chapter.

Jimmie (Dick) is a big fan of Merriwell's. He has just been given a baseball by Frank and seen him off for a baseball game and is playing with his dog. When Jimmie throws a baseball for the dog to fetch a car hits the dog. Frank rushes back to take the dog for medical care, saying getting help for the dog is more important than the game. That wins him more adulation from Jimmie and sets the tone for the entire serial. Frank is always missing some sporting event—at which he is billed as the hero—because he stops to save someone.

The dog's prognosis must be good because when Frank and Elsie drop

Jimmie (Dick Jones) smiles his thanks as Frank Merriwell (Don Briggs) gives him a baseball.

Jimmie back at home before racing for the game Jimmie is smiling. That's the last seen of Dickie in this serial.

House Peters, Jr. is Merriwell's same team rival for acclaim. Peters would later work with Dick on the *Buffalo Bill, Jr.*, and *The Range Rider* TV series, and the Gene Autry feature, *The Old West*.

Dick was not always thrilled with the scenes he played.

One scene was so corny—admiring his baseball or something like that.

Dick's first major serial role came before he reached his tenth birthday.

For *Blake of Scotland Yard*, he received fifth billing, with his face as one of the head shots in the front titles of each chapter.

Blake was a typical low-budget, mid-1930s serial, full of action, and lacking in production values.

Sir James Blake (Herbert Rawlinson), in an effort to promote world peace, backs the creation of a machine (think laser) that can wipe out any battle force at a distance, therefore making the armed forces of the nations obsolete.

Jerry Sheehan (Ralph Byrd), and Hope Mason (Joan Barclay), who is Sir James' niece, come up with the Death Ray. Dick plays Hope's brother, Bobby, who is rapidly learning American slang from Jerry, to the dismay of his Uncle Jimmie. Blake's difficulty with understanding American slang becomes a running joke throughout the serial.

The mysterious Scorpion, an international criminal, and his cohorts are out to steal the ray for their own nefarious purposes. The end of every chapter holds a promise to reveal the identity of the Scorpion in the next week's chapter but, of course, it is Chapter Fifteen before we learn the identity of the despicable villain hidden behind the mask and the claw glove.

The Scorpion stood out in Dick's memory.

I think they double billed that thing. The Scorpion *was another title they had on it. The Scorpion had a claw-like hand that would come sneaking out of the corners to try to grab me. I had a lot of dialog with Ralph Byrd and Herbert Rawlinson.*

I was fascinated by all the crazy electronic equipment they would put together, like in the funny papers but big stuff that would be more noticeable in motion pictures; stuff that had arcs and sparks flying out. They had all kinds of funny stuff that would make all kinds of noises. They wouldn't do anything or build anything, just give a shock. That's all. It was another job.

Standard cliffhanger serial though it might have been, *Blake of Scotland Yard* offered challenge and opportunity for young Dickie.

One of the more unique aspects of this thriller is how totally Bobby is a partner with the adults. Though from time to time Uncle Jimmie will tell

The Scorpion creeps up on Hope (Joan Barclay) and Bobby (Dick Jones).

Jerry, "Take care of the children," meaning Hope and Bobby, Bobby takes action and makes important decisions on his own. And the adults respect that.

His inclusion begins with the first chapter when he is allowed to witness a demonstration of the Death Ray along with the representatives of international military forces. He is formally decked out in the Lord Fauntleroy suit that he remembered with distaste but soon he swaps it for day clothes more suitable for the action to come.

Perhaps his presence was geared to keep the front-row kids in the audience more involved. Certainly watching a nine-year-old (Dick's age at the time) perform daring acts and help track down the villains would keep the kids coming back to see one of their own save the day rather than having to be rescued at the end of the chapter.

His exploits are impressive and it is easy to imagine all the front-row kids glued to the screen thinking, "Yeah! That's what I'd do," as they watched Dick tackling the baddies.

From Chapter One, when he escapes by tackling Daggett, the butler, who was assigned to take him to his room to avoid the villains, Bobby is part of the crime fighting. He is returned to safety by Dr. Marshall (Lloyd Hughes) only to escape again. The action is over by the time he reaches the scene, but later in the chapter he does get into a tussle with one of the Scorpion's henchmen. As the chapter ends, he demonstrates his ability to faint when locked in an airless vault.

Hope (Joan Barclay) and Bobby (Dick Jones) watch the action before they are captured and locked in the vault.

In the next chapter, he proves that he can take and identify fingerprints. With that skill he determines that a note delivered to his sister that is purported to be from Sir James is a forgery, because his uncle's prints are nowhere on the paper.

By Chapter Three, Hope has been suckered to Paris by the fake note and

Bobby is left at the home, Mallow Hall, to hold the fort, so to speak. He is smart enough to realize that Sir James has been coerced to call home and give him instructions. Therefore, he alters the directions to foil the villains, and then follows them.

The Scorpion is furious and in the next chapter chews out his henchmen for allowing themselves to be trailed to the hideout "by a child." Bobby is captured but still manages to hide the radium tubes necessary for the Death Ray to work from the baddies and escape.

Bobby had to hide the radium tubes in the closet of his captors' hideout and locating the hideout for Blake before the villains discover the hiding place is his next challenge. As it turned out, he hid the tubes in a pencil in the pocket of the Scorpion's vest.

What the Scorpion doesn't know can't hurt the good guys.

The Scorpion kidnaps Bobby from Mallow Hall and returns him to his hideout. Faking sleep, Bobby sends the Scorpion on a wild goose chase back to the Hall and in the process manages to slyly snag the pencil holding the radium tubes from the Scorpion's pocket. The Scorpion leaves his captive with some of his henchmen and heads for Mallow Hall.

Meanwhile, Blake rescues his nephew but is overpowered. While he fights Bobby calls Scotland Yard so that Inspector Henderson (Sam Flint) and his men arrive on the scene in the nick of time. All return to the Hall in hopes of capturing the Scorpion.

In the next chapter, Bobby returns the favor by rescuing his uncle from an explosion in the tunnels under the Hall. Baron Polinka (Jimmy Aubrey) visits Blake while he is recuperating and Bobby's facial expressions and body language expressing his distrust of the Baron are dead on target. When Polinka leaves, Bobby stows away in his car in an effort to gather evidence against him.

Charles (Frank Wayne), the butler who replaced Daggett when it was learned he was part of the Scorpion's gang, tells Sir James that Bobby concealed himself in the car. Blake approves, saying, "That boy knows what he is doing."

In trailing Polinka, Bobby ends up near the Scorpion's hideout and sees Count Basil Segaloff (William Farrell), whom we know to be a baddie, go to a meeting with the Scorpion. He follows and hears them making a deal for the Death Ray. Bobby doesn't know that his uncle has set a trap and is masquerading as the Scorpion. The real Scorpion arrives before the trap is sprung. Bobby helps the police break into the room but not before the Scorpion escapes with the Death Ray.

However, Bobby can now tell Blake and the Inspector where Count Segaloff hangs out.

Back at Mallow Hall, Bobby states his theory about the location of the Death Ray to Hope, Jerry and Dr. Marshall. He believes that the Scorpion has hidden it in the underground passages below Mallow Hall.

Hope (Joan Barclay) and Bobby (Dick Jones) decide to search the underground passages for the Death Ray.

Cliffhanging

Without telling anyone, Bobby and Hope decide to search the tunnels. They discover someone has removed the batteries from the flashlights but continue to wander until Hope says she thinks they are lost. Bobby replies, "Don't worry, Hope. I'm doing a good job of that."

They find the Death Ray but are unable to escape with it. It's worth noting that Bobby has a good fight in the tunnel with one of the baddies.

The Scorpion and gang grab the Death Ray and run to a waiting car that will take them to an airstrip where a plane waits to fly them to Paris. They take the Death Ray to sell to Count Segaloff. The adults pursue them, leaving Bobby behind with instructions to keep an eye on Charles.

It takes the adults two chapters to retrieve the Death Ray and bring it and themselves back to England.

One of the Scorpion's henchmen captures Bobby (Dick Jones).

When they arrive back at Mallow Hall, Bobby greets them with the announcement that he has just discovered an acid that will eat through anything. He is alone in one of the rooms when one of the Scorpion's men captures him and takes him to the underground passages.

The Scorpion is in the process of setting a charge of dynamite to blow up the Hall where a meeting of the Anti-War Society is scheduled to meet at 2 p.m. He is most unhappy that his henchman grabbed Bobby and brought him below.

When Bobby was captured, he lifted his captor's gun and pretended to have fainted. Thus, the villains are not paying attention to him as they finish the job of setting the charge. Bobby pulls the gun on them, but just as he demands that the Scorpion unmask, another henchman comes into the room and grabs him from behind.

Bobby (Dick Jones), left tied up by the Scorpion's henchmen in the same room with the explosives set to blow up the mansion, works his way to the fuse and tugs it free from the charge with his teeth before escaping.

The villains leave him tied up and tied to the wall by the fireplace with the fuse burning across the room. They emptied his pockets, leaving the bottle of acid on the mantel. Bobby squirms and wiggles until he is able to tump the bottle with his feet and start a drip of acid. He maneuvers the rope holding him to the wall so that the acid cuts through it.

As soon as he can move, he ooches across the room and pulls the fuse loose from the dynamite with his teeth. Then he works his way back to the acid drip and frees his hands. (In other cliffhangers, many adults did not do similar scenes as well as Dick did in this one.)

Meanwhile the Anti-War Society is meeting upstairs. Jerry is about to demonstrate that the machine is safely back in the right hands and working properly when Bobby dashes into the room to reveal what has happened. (Be sure to keep an eye out for Dick's wowing athletic leap as he enters the room.) Jerry looks on the machine's screen and sees the villains on the hill outside the mansion watching for the explosion.

Blake, Jerry and the Inspector go after them, leaving Hope, Bobby and some guards there with the machine. The henchman who had captured Bobby shoots Sir James. Hope cries out but Bobby tells her the man couldn't kill Uncle Jimmie because he removed the lead from the bullets in that gun when he was captured. (What front-row kid in the theater would not want to share in saving the day with Bobby?)

Back at the Hall, Baron Polinka teargases Hope, Bobby and the guards and steals the Death Ray.

Blake and Jerry come back to find them laid out in the floor. They, along with Henderson and his men from the Yard, go into London, to the house where Segaloff was staying. Sir James masquerades as the porter in the house. In a confrontation they capture some of the gang and do away with others but still others get away.

At Mallow Hall, Hope and Bobby are awakened by a noise and see the Scorpion lurking. They jump into a car and follow him to London, to the place where Sir James and Jerry are.

Two Scorpions show up. A terrific fight ensues and Bobby, with an impressive leap over the banister, chases the Scorpion who is running away with the Death Ray.

In the next battle, that Scorpion gets away but Blake retrieves the Death Ray and they all go back to Mallow Hall for the standard Chapter Fourteen review of the story, which consists mainly of flashbacks.

Bobby (Dick Jones, right) explains his theory to Inspector Henderson (Sam Flint, left) and Sir James (Herbert Rawlinson, center).

With the final chapter coming up, another trap is set for the Scorpion. This time it works.

The Scorpion is revealed and finally captured. In the final scenes, Bobby is, once more, in his Lord Fauntleroy outfit as Sir James delivers the Death Ray machine to the custody of the League of Nations.

Dick wasn't happy with some aspects of the serial.

In Blake of Scotland Yard, *I had to emulate an English accent. Me, with a Texas drawl, coming up with an English accent and dressing like Little Lord*

Fauntleroy. I wasn't too happy working in that one. It was just another job and I got it done—got it over with as quick as I could.

Bobby (Dick Jones, front center) admires the invention made by Jerry Sheehan (Ralph Byrd, from left) and his sister Hope (Joan Barclay) as his uncle Sir James Blake (Herbert Rawlinson) appreciate his comments. Note Dick's costume in this scene.

It's interesting that Dick chiefly remembered this for the fussiness of his first and last chapter costume and the British accent he worked to create. (He was, by the way, the only cast member who worked at it.) His role is major and his character is a key player in several of the twists. His fights are good. This was a 1930s serial with fights of that era that had none of the finesse nor realism of the later fight sequences such as those that filled *The Range Rider* and *Buffalo Bill, Jr.* but Dick was in some fight sequences.

Something interesting about *Blake of Scotland Yard* is the number of performers with whom Dick would share billing in other shows. Mentioning a few would include: Sam Flint, who played Inspector Henderson, Blake's contact at Scotland Yard, later appeared in two *Range Rider* episodes, "Western Edition" and "Two-Fisted Justice." Dick Curtis was also in *Range Riders*, as was George DeNormand. Bruce Bennett, uncredited but one of the Scorpion's henchmen, had the male lead in *Flying Fists*, though he was billed as Herman Brix in that one. Dick would also share other cast listings with Ralph Byrd and Herbert Rawlinson.

Also a notable goof is that in Chapter Twelve, when Jerry runs in to revive Hope, he calls her Joan, the name of the actress who played Hope Mason.

Watching Dick more than hold his own with adult actors makes it a fun watch, one his fans will appreciate far more than Dick did.

Hail, Hail, the Gang's All Here

THE *OUR GANG* COMEDIES HAVE BEEN BILLED as the all-time best kids shows ever filmed. Though Dick wasn't part of the regular crew, he worked in several of the famous shorts.

He reflected on what stuck with him in general from the experience:

I remember a few things that stood out from the Our Gang *comedies because that was a long time ago and I only worked on them spasmodically, whereas the regular group worked constantly.*

There was a schoolhouse at Roach Studios, and they were in there all the time when they were shooting. I would be there and I would come in. They liked to work me during the summertime when there wasn't any school so they could cut the time I had to spend with the social worker.

They didn't like me because I'd always disappear. I liked going out in the back lot and playing on the old sailing ships they had there.

Though the title claims otherwise, Dick's final picture of 1935 was the short, *Our Gang Follies of 1936*. Like every other film of the year in which he wasn't someone "as a boy," his character's name was Dickie.

The plotline goes like this. The Gang is putting on a show. The anticipated act is The Flory Dory Sixtet, but they are no-shows. They were third on the bill, right after Darla sings, but are quickly moved to after the dance of the skeletons. Then more singing replaces the group. After this the audience begins to chant. "We want the Flory Dories." Spanky comes up with the idea of the boys dressing in the girls' costumes and pretending to be The Flory Dory Sixtet. Greeted by protests that they don't know the dance, Spanky insists that he knows what to do.

Dick remembered:

I worked on Our Gang Follies of 1936. *In that one, first I'm a stagehand, then I'm part of an act. We were the Flory Dory Girls Sixtet and following Spanky.*

We got in the girls' costumes, and Spanky told us all to do what he did. We were imitating him, and a monkey got in the bustle with a needle and was sticking Spanky with the hat pin. The monkey would jab Spanky and every time he'd jump we all did follow the leader. I was the last one in line on that one. [Actually, Dick is the one immediately behind Spanky.]

The monkey that had been running back and forth across the stage jumps into Spanky's bustle with a hatpin in its hand just as the boys go on stage. As Dick said, Spanky jumps, the other boys jump, too. Spanky wiggles, they wiggle, until finally they wiggle out of their skirts, ending the show.

Dick served in several capacities in *Our Gang Follies of 1936*. He can be seen valiantly pulling the curtain. He also appears in a skeleton suit after the bones dance number and then does his part following Spanky in the ill-fated Flory Dory routine.

Dick, Alfalfa, Buckwheat, and Darla pose for a publicity still for the *Our Gang Follies of 1936*.

Young Dickie was a good dancer and showed off his dance ability occasionally in *Our Gang* shows.

I was with a group that did shows at the Orpheum Theater downtown and other places and performed in Our Gang *comedies. I tap danced a lot.*

One I remember was a big production where we were all dressed up in tux and tails and top hats.

This was the early 1936 short, *The Pinch Singer*. In it, the Gang hopes to win the $50 prize offered for the best child act in a radio station sponsored competition. Members of the Gang try out to choose the most likely winner with Alfalfa attempting to disguise himself in several costumes to get his song selected. Darla, tiny and with light brown/dark blonde hair, wins the opportunity to represent them.

The scene shifts to the radio station with Spanky pacing the floor, as the time to perform nears with no Darla in sight. When Spanky goes to find Darla, Alfalfa begins to pace.

Three acts perform before Alfalfa becomes the pinch singer: a male saxophone trio; a vocal group of two boys and a girl in blackface singing "Has Anybody Seen My Gal?"; and a male singer backed by four tap-dancing couples performing to "Broadway Melody." Dick is one of the dancers. In his top hat and tails with feet flying, he's part of a group of child dancers of the style and talent it's hard to find in this century. He sparkles in his fancy formal tux with showy tapping and a big smile. He must have appealed to the cameraman, too, because that grin and a roll of the eye got a close-up before the camera panned back to display those talented toes.

The radio audience decides the victor, so when The Gang members hear Alfalfa filling in for the missing Darla, they run to the phones to vote. Naturally, Alfalfa wins in the end.

Dick's most prominent role in the *Our Gang* shorts came in 1937 with *The Pigskin Palooka*. It was a shift of character, for he was neither saving the day nor a lad in trouble, but the mischievous Spike, out to defeat the Gang in football using whatever devious methods necessary.

Alfalfa writes home that he's a big football star at school. Of course he's never played a game in his life. Darla organizes the Gang to welcome home the hero Alfalfa, whom they hope will save their team from the Tigers in the Saturday game.

Dick leads Spike's Tigers. He tries every way fair and foul to keep Spanky's All-Stars from winning but, of course, through one fortunate accident after another, the All-Stars win.

Dick tells it:

In Pigskin Palooka, *I was the baddie. I got a big wad of gum and stuck it on the ball and Alfalfa couldn't get it off his hand. When he went to pass the ball he couldn't pass it.*

I had a good part.

Spike (Dick Jones, right center) threatens Alfalfa (center), as Spanky (just left of Alfalfa) and The Gang look on.

Gordon Douglas directed *The Pigskin Palooka*. Dick respected Douglas very much.

The *Our Gang Follies of 1938* was another "we've got a barn, we've got talent; let's have a show" Our Gang short.

In this one, all the girls want Alfalfa to croon, but he's decided to sing opera. Spanky begs him to croon for the audience, but he refuses and goes out to find a producer to hire him to sing opera. The opera producer (Henry Brandon), waggishly gives him a contract to perform in twenty years, and Alfalfa triumphantly returns to flaunt his contract in Spanky's face and take a nap.

To sleep, perchance to dream. In Alfalfa's dream, Spanky's prediction of him starving and singing opera on the street comes true. Spanky has a nightclub and the Gang members—except for the stray Alfalfa—perform and make, as a now dark-haired Darla says, "hundreds and thousands of dollars."

Dick (at curtain) and Porky (right) watch as Alfalfa (right of Dick) triumphantly tells Spanky he has a contract to sing opera.

Dick is the curtain puller when the Gang is in present time, and can be seen as part of the upper class, tux-wearing group of dancers in "The Love Bug'll Get You If You Don't Watch Out/You're the One for Me" production number at Club Spanky in Alfalfa's dream.

Dick's time with The Gang was limited. The most fun part of watching him in *Our Gang* shorts is appreciating his dance ability. The same balance and athleticism that made his action work so impressive, gave him a natural gift for dancing. He's cute in the follies shorts and prominent in *The Pigskin Palooka*, but catching a glimpse of his tapping toes, easy swing, and charming grin makes *The Pinch Singer* the one to seek out.

Go West, Young Man

DICK'S FIRST FORAY INTO THE GENRE with which many of his fans identify him—the Western—came in his second year of filmmaking. He was in three Westerns in that year, *Westward Ho*, *Trail of the Hawk*, and *Moonlight on the Prairie*.

Republic's *Westward Ho*, another film in which Dick grew up to be an adult in the story, has him turning into Frank McGlynn, Jr. (Jim Wyatt), after the first minutes. The director was Robert North Bradbury. Dick's credit was "Jim Wyatt as a boy." The star was a young John Wayne. (Bradley Metcalfe played John Wyatt as a boy.)

The boys' family is headed west with wagons and a large herd of cattle. Mark Wyatt (Hank Bell) has decided to quit hauling freight and settle with his wife and two young sons. As they roll along, young Jim tells his brother he wants to see some action. When John says he likes the song the hands are singing (good cowboy harmony, "Westward Ho"), Jim calls it flat. He likes soldiers' music better. He doesn't like school. He complains that he has seen neither Indians nor bandits. He wants to see bad men.

The bandits materialize all too soon, when they raid the wagons. Jim tries to fire the gun he's holding, but the kick throws him back into the wagon bed. Both parents are killed, and John left for dead. Jim has crawled to the back of the wagon. He points the gun at the bandits and tells them to put up their hands. Ballard (Jack Curtis), the leader of the outlaw band, likes the little fellow's brashness and tells Red (Yakima Canutt) to bring him along. Red snatches him from the wagon and carries him off.

That's Dick's last appearance in this movie.

In spite of his young age and limited screen time, Dick remembered this one.

I worked with Yakima Canutt in 1935. John Wayne picture. The outlaws came in, hijacked the wagon train, kidnapped me. Yak jerked me out of the covered wagon and rode off with me and the next thing you know I'd grown up and was a different actor.

It took me from '35—well, almost twenty years—to get even with him. I caught up with him in Rocky Mountain *and shot him dead. I told Yakima Canutt, "It took me twenty years to get even with you." He took me out of the wagon and kidnapped me and I shot him in* Rocky Mountain *and told him, "I finally got even with you." And he said, "I don't even know what you're talking about."*

Dick criticized his performance.

Westward Ho. *When I watch it, I can't understand what I say. Close up where we're riding in the boot of the wagon and I've got a gun and I say I'm going to shoot Indians or something like that. I can't understand what I'm saying. Dumb kid mumbles all the time.*

Red (Yakima Canutt) looks at bandit leader Ballard (Jack Curtis) to make sure he is not joking when he tells him to bring young Jim Wyatt along with them.

Close up taken from worn photo of Dick Jones as Jim Wyatt.

These boots he danced in, the first custom-made boots he ever owned, were a prized possession. Dick had them bronzed and they were kept in the den at his house until he died.

In *Trail of the Hawk* aka *The Hawk,* Dick not only had to ride but also to call on his dance skills. The film was the one starring role for Yancey Lane. Young Dickie was a charmer in this film even if the film is not widely known. He received third billing behind Lane and the female lead, Betty Jordan.

Dick played Dickie Thomas, the brother of the heroine. Lane is John King, the son of the ranch owner, but unable to prove it because the villain (The Hawk) stole his proof. Dick turns in a memorable performance that includes a tap dance routine in the bunk house.

Dick described *Trail of the Hawk* as a one-hit wonder.

Trail of the Hawk *with a guy named Yancey Lane was a four- or five-day wonder. It had a real tight budget. That was it—Yancey Lane's one picture.*

I did a tap dance routine in that Western and I thought they messed up my cowboy boots when they put taps on the toes and the heels but I've still got that pair of boots and I've got them bronzed and they're in my den. That was my first pair of tailor-made boots—hand-made boots.

The tap dance routine was in the bunkhouse with all the cowboys whooping and hollerin' and clapping.

Dickie Thomas (Dick Jones), Jeff Murdock (Rollo Dix) and Jim King (Lafe McKee) watch as Jack King/Jay Price (Yancey Lane) is revived by Betty Thomas (Betty Jordan) after being injured saving Dickie from being stomped by a horse. Note: Dick has a dorky little hat in this film.

Trail of the Hawk was another one of those movies with a crew of stupid townsmen and sheriff. Jay Price's (Yancey Lane) mother tells him his real name is Jack King and his father sends a registered letter for him to all the post offices in the area hoping to find the son she took away from him. He makes a promise to her on her death bed that he will return to his father. After she's dead and buried, he goes to claim the letter. The sheriff and postmaster, who have known him for years as an honest person, don't believe his story. They know his mother just died, after a private conversation between the two before her death, but refuse to believe him. He steals the letter, and rides off with a posse on his trail, accompanied by his faithful canine companion, Zandra.

On his way to his father's ranch, he comes upon a meeting between The Hawk and his segundo. He hides and listens to the plans.

Jack rides up to the ranch just as Tony the cook (Don Orlando), the comic element in the film, is trying to ride a bucking horse. Dick, perched on the fence, hangs himself up as he cheers and Jack rushes to his rescue.

As Dickie says, "Thanks, mister. Guess you kinda saved my life."

Dick is a key player in *Trail of the Hawk*. At only seven years old, his role is pivotal for many of the plot turns. He and his sister Betty (Betty Jordan in her only credited film) are foster children of Jack's father (Lafe McKee).

Dick is a little imp in this one, harassing the cook—especially infuriating Tony by wanting to shoot an apple off his head William Tell style, popping people with his slingshot, pulling pranks then hiding to laugh.

Dickie (center) interrupts a touching moment between Jay/Jack (Yancey Lane) and his sister (Betty Jordan).

However, he shows his chops in some terrific scenes: competing with Jack at shooting—Dickie with his slingshot, Jack with his gun; riding—obviously Dick on the horse; teasing Jack about his shy romance with Betty; informing his sister that Jack is wanted by the law back home; rescuing Jack when The Hawk captures him.

Dickie unties Jay/Jack after he has been captured by The Hawk.

Plenty of older people appeared on the screen who were far less effective actors than seven-year-old Dick.

Even though Dick regards his tap dance in the bunkhouse as corny, "dumb," and "stupid," it's a delight to watch. Every Dick Jones fan should see this one.

Safety restrictions on what child actors could or could not do were not as strict in the 1930s. Though social workers and studio teachers were a presence, if a kid could ride, then it was permissible for that kid to do just that. (Dick was not alone in this. As one watches the old B-Westerns, several child riders stand out, among them Dick's friend, Buzz Henry, who can be seen pelting across the prairie on a horse at age five.)

Tony (Don Orlando), Jay/Jack (Yancey Lane), Dick, Jeff (Rollo Dix) and musicians sing in the bunkhouse in this publicity shot.

I got a lot of jobs in Westerns because they always seemed to want a kid to ride a horse, and I had no problem there, and they didn't have to double me. To double me, they'd have to get a little girl that was over eighteen, or a guy that was real little that was over eighteen because they didn't want to have to pay for two social workers. It was an advantage in Westerns. I didn't even have to go on interviews. They'd just call and say we've got a job here for you.

Moonlight on the Prairie featured seven-and-a-half-year-old Dick in a prominent role.

Ace Andrews (Dick Foran) is falsely accused of the murder of the father of Dickie Roberts (Dick Jones). The man was a brute, and Dickie's mother, Barbara (Sheila Mannors/Bromley), had taken the boy east to live. When notified of her husband's death, she brings the boy back to claim his inheritance.

Her problem is that she has a limited time, and the real murderers have taken care to make sure no one in the area will help her and her son reach the ranch in time.

Ace and his buddy, Small Change (George E. Stone), come to her rescue. They uncover many discrepancies in the way the ranch has been run, and in the end, win out.

Impressive for Dick Jones fans will be the scene in which Dick does a saddle fall from a mule. It's obviously Dick, not a double, something that couldn't happen in twenty-first century Hollywood without wires and a green screen.

Even though his character is one of those screen kids who unintentionally aides and abets the baddies, Dick does a terrific job with lines, facial expressions, and believability. Bluntly, he shows off his not-insignificant acting chops—at seven-and-a-half years old.

Dick remembered the picture fondly.

Moonlight on the Prairie was a fun picture. That was with Dick Foran, and that picture was Wild Bill Elliott's first cowboy picture. Before this, he was a dress extra, and he always had a pencil-thin mustache. He was the sheriff. I remember that very well because the next time I saw him he was in The Great Adventures of Wild Bill Hickok *that we made up in Kanab.*

Dick Foran shouldn't have been cast as a cowboy. He had a great baritone voice, and cowboys didn't sing like that. I remember one time that he was supposed to go running into a stirrup mount and get on his horse real fast, and after about the fifth take he turned around and said, "I just can't get my fat ass up on this horse."

In my opinion, that was a great job, because we rode up in June Lake Circle, up in the High Sierras. There are three lakes up there and we went from one to the other. The scenery was great. I loved it up there, and I got to do another stunt that I got adjusted for.

When the stampede of horses came down, I was on this damned donkey that would cue to spin around and then fall down, and I had to do that right in front of the stampede of horses. Bob Woodward, the stuntman, was doubling Dick Foran and he comes and picks me up and gets me out of the way. There's another one where I was the cliffhanger.

In Moonlight on the Prairie *they had me ride that damned spotted Shetland pony.* [Actually, his Shetland was not spotted in this film. It looks like a bay.] *I hate Shetland ponies because they are so spoiled and got that mind of their own. You want to go left. They want to go right. You want to go right. They want to go left. You want to giddee-up. They want to sit down.*

The director on Moonlight on the Prairie *was Ross Lederman, who did a lot of* Range Riders *and* Buffalo Bill, Jrs. *He was one of the best for the stuff we were doing. He knew Westerns; he knew how to get the scenery in; and he knew action.*

The next year, Dick appeared in *Daniel Boone*, starring George O'Brien. As a young man, O'Brien had starred in the silent Western, *The Iron Horse*, directed by an also young John Ford. His career spanned many years and a variety of genres. *Daniel Boone* is reported to be one of O'Brien's personal favorites of the films in which he appeared.

From today's point of view, it is a fairly standard frontier Western, but Dick did have a death scene, which he performed credibly.

I worked on Daniel Boone *with George O'Brien. He was a nice guy. He had a barrel chest like it wouldn't quit. He was bigger around in the chest than he was from feet to hair.*

We shot that up at Big Bear, and they built a regular fort up there in the dry lake part of Big Bear Lake. It was quite interesting.

I remember Heather Angel better than George O'Brien. She was supposed to be my sister.

That's another time I had a damn Shetland pony.

I remember Clarence Muse. I remember a scene when I'm out chasing Daniel Boone to warn him, or something like that, and John Carradine comes along and takes a shot at him and misses him and hits me. And I get dead.

Clarence Muse comes and picks me up and sings a beautiful song—it brings tears to my eyes just thinking about it—"Make Way, Gotta Travel"—and there's a long travel shot where he's walking along, singing the song, and they cut it out of the movie. I cried all the time he was carrying me and they had to cut it because I was supposed to be dead. They show him carrying me, but they cut the sound out.

In *Land Beyond the Law*, Chip Douglas (Dick Foran) is a wild but good-hearted young rascal, who has split with his father and works for Slade Henaberry (Cy Kendall), a big rancher, who supports "extra" activities by his hands, including trying to run off the nesters. When Chip's father is killed in a raid on his herd, Chip moves to the side of law and order and agrees to become the sheriff of Bitter Creek.

Dick has the role of one of the nester's sons, Bobby Skinner, but *Land Beyond the Law* left him with a total blank. Even with film "refreshers," it is as if the movie did not exist, yet there he is. Even with the film showing to jog his memory, Dick did not remember making this film. He has only a few lines with Foran. Dick was probably only eight or nine at the time, so it is not surprising that this one did not leave an imprint on him.

Dick insisted:

I don't remember working with Dick Foran but once. A friend gave me a copy of the tape and I still don't remember it.

Dick's admiration for Kermit Maynard, the star of *Wild Horse Round-Up*, was shared by the people of the film business as a whole. The film was one of a series of Maynard's "outdoor" movies for Ambassador Pictures. Low budget, high action—nothing in it stood out for young Dick Jones but the personality of the star.

The only remembrance I have of Wild Horse Round-Up *is that I liked Kermit Maynard a whole bunch. He made Ken Maynard look good because he did all of Ken Maynard's horseback riding—trick riding, stuff like that.*

Kermit was great. I admired him. When he found out he wasn't going to be star status, he immediately got himself an extras card and kept on working and just kept on working. He was in about thirty percent of The Range Riders *and at least twenty-five percent of the* Buffalo Bill Jrs. *as a riding extra. Always in the background and very, very quiet. You wouldn't even know he was around. He was another nice guy. One of the good guys.*

There were a couple of scenes they did on the stage that were supposed to be outside and that was like fingernails on a chalkboard. It rankled me to do that because you could tell the difference in the sound and it just wasn't like being outdoors.

I think that's why I gravitated to Westerns because I liked being outdoors. I didn't like being indoors.

Jack Benson (Kermit Maynard) brings young Dickie Williams (Dick Jones) back to the ranch after his horse has run away.

In *Wild Horse Round-Up*, Charlie Doan (John Merton) knows the railroad plans to run a line through Wild Horse Valley and is acquiring all the land—chiefly by foul means. He sends his night riders to burn out many of the ranchers, but holds off on Ruth Williams (Beth Marion, billed as Betty Lloyd) and her brother Dickie's ranch. He wants the ranch *and* Ruth. Jack

Benson (Kermit Maynard) and his pals ride into the valley and come to Ruth and Dickie's aid.

Dickie Williams (Dick Jones) asks Jack Benson (Kermit Maynard) if he is afraid as Benson prepares to break the wild stallion, Black Satan, in order to help Dickie's sister, Ruth, keep the ranch.

Dick received third billing and had a fun role in this film. He's a feisty little thing. After "capturing" Jack and his men, he takes a real shine to the newcomers. The scene in which he gets the drop on the singing bunch (the singing obviously dubbed), then herds them back to his sister at gunpoint is delightful. With no comic sidekick, he provides humor by hauling around a rifle just slightly shorter than he is tall and doing all in his power to kindle romance between Jack and his sister. This show without Dick's performance would be flat, despite some nice chase sequences.

An interesting note is that one member of Maynard's singing band is Dick Curtis, sometimes called the "Meanest Man in Hollywood." It's refreshing to

A lobby card for *Wild Horse Round-Up* with a posed still of Dick Jones, Kermit Maynard, and Beth Marion (billed here as Betty Lloyd).

watch this chronic villain in a light, good-guy role. He would later work with Dick in *The Range Rider* before his early death in 1952.

Dickie's role in *Renfrew of the Royal Mounted* had little time for development. He played Tommy MacDonald, son of Corporal MacDonald (Donald Reed), who is killed early on by the Indian ally of the baddies (Chief Thundercloud). However, a still from his tearful scene made one of the lobby cards.

Dick reflected:

The only reason I got that part, I guess, is because I could cry at the drop of a hat. They thought I was a fine little actor because I could cry. I would think about a dog story that came out of a book.

His ability to cry on cue certainly had to be the key factor in obtaining this role. Just about all he does is cry. When his father is killed, he sobs on the body and is later comforted by Renfrew—still in tears.

Sergeant Renfrew (James Newill) comforts Tommy MacDonald (Dick Jones) after the death of his father.

From left: Lane Chandler, John Merton, Bruce Bennett, Ernie Adams, Jack Randall, and Dick in front with rifle in a posed still from *Land of Fighting Men*.

His only other scenes are at the Mounties' picnic, when he has an exchange with Sergeant Renfrew, saying he doesn't want to grow up to be a Mountie, but a G-Man. He changes his tune after his father's death and then wants to be a Mountie, just like his dad. Once he makes that decision, still tearful, we see him no more in the film.

Land of Fighting Men, a 1938 Jack Randall Western, is one of the lost films of the era. The master copy was destroyed in a storage building fire, and Dick was still hunting a personal copy of it at the time of his death. He had fourth billing in this film and enjoyed making it.

Dick told me:

Everybody says that one's going to be impossible to get unless somebody got a copy of the thing when it was out on the road in theaters. The original was lost in a fire in PRC's storage over on Melrose.

That's just like trying to find that five minutes in This Gun for Hire. *Somebody somewhere's got a 16 mm copy that was used when they showed it out in the hinterlands in the small theaters.*

When Dick and I first met at the 1987 Memphis Film Festival, I asked him about the cowboy hero's hero, Buck Jones. He told me, "He was all that you wanted him to be."

I worked with Buck Jones in two pictures. The first was Smoke Tree Range. *My chief memory from that one is the dorky little hat I had to wear. That was just like the hat they put on me in* The Strawberry Roan. *I hated that.*

Muriel Evans was the lady in that one. She was a real supporter of the Motion Picture and Television Hospital. She has a couple of murals there—maybe three-by-five—with umpteen jillion pictures of her in them. In one of them, there are two pictures from Smoke Tree Range *of us together. And in one of those my face is about three-by-five size.*

She was real nice to me. When she moved from her apartment to Motion Picture her gentleman friend brought over a whole bunch of stuff that she had saved—pictures and stuff. I was in some of them.

*S*moke Tree Range had a fairly typical B-Western plot.

Teddy Page (Dick Jones) and his sister Nan (Muriel Evans) are kidnapped by El Capitan's henchmen. This picture was included in one of the murals.

Lee Cary (Buck Jones, center) manhandles Gil Hawkins (Ted Adams) and orders him away from Teddy (Dick Jones) and Nan Page (Muriel Evans).

Lee Cary (Buck Jones) and his grandfather Jim (John Elliott) don't see eye to eye on the way to run the Smoke Tree. Grandfather wants to run out the nesters, including Nan Page (Muriel Evans) and her brother Teddy (Dick Jones). Jim doesn't know that they are niece and nephew of Bill Page, who disappeared under suspicious circumstances, and are his heirs.

Lee and Nan meet when her horse throws her and he comes to the rescue. They get along famously until she discovers he's tied to the Smoke Tree.

Nevertheless, he becomes her protector and stops one of his grandfather's men from running them off Las Posas, the ranch which is rightfully theirs.

Meanwhile, El Capitan is raiding all the ranches in the area. Lee's job becomes double—to see that the Pages retain what belongs to them and find and eliminate El Capitan.

Dick doesn't have a lot of screen time in *Smoke Tree Range*, so it isn't surprising that his striking memory is the hat he was forced to wear. That would especially stick in the mind of a child when compared to the classic wide-brimmed hat worn by Buck Jones.

Dick's more vivid memories of Jones come from the second movie they made together, *Hollywood Round-Up*.

The first time I was at the Memphis Film Festival (1987), I was able to chase down somebody who had a good copy of that one. That was the first time I'd been able to see it.

Buck Jones was one hell of a good cowboy. I thought he was a great cowboy. He was a better action guy on horseback than most of them. At that point Bobby Woodward was doubling him. That's the same Bob Woodward who we had on The Range Rider. *Buck Jones was getting up in years but he was still handy.*

Hollywood Round-Up is one of a number of movies about making movies. Grant Drexel (Grant Withers) is the conceited star. Buck Kennedy (Buck Jones) is the stuntman. Carol Stevens (Helen Twelvetrees) hasn't been making money for her studio, so she is loaned out for a Western. She's horrified to be playing in a "horse opera," but she likes the handy stuntman.

Her little brother, Dickie (Dick Jones), meets Buck first and has a fun scene with Buck and Silver. Silver shows off his tricks and Dickie films it with the "swell" camera his sister gave him for his birthday.

Buck and Grant (Note: The top-billed male characters have the same first names as the actors who play them—Buck, Grant, Dickie.) have a confrontation over the way Drexel treats the lady and immediately the star has it in for his stuntman. Dickie wasn't there at the time, but he gets the picture on cowboy hero Grant Drexel when he wants to film him with his fancy camera and Drexel rebuffs him.

The entire crew, including Dickie, go on location, and soon, Buck and Grant clash again over Carol. Buck is fired.

Dickie is preparing to stay with Buck while his sister goes out with the crew to film, when Buck is approached by the "producer" of a new film company that wants to hire him. The new film company is a gang of bank robbers setting Buck up to take the fall. Dickie runs off to tell Carol that Buck will be staying in Cornville. By the time they return, Buck is in jail for holding up the bank, and the robbers are on the way to Mexico.

Dickie can't leave his hero in jail. That night, he saddles horses for himself and Buck and appears at the window of Buck's cell. That little face pushed between the bars with his hat flattened into a frame is a memorable image.

Buck scolds him and tells him to go back to bed but Dickie persists in feeding him information until Buck says, "I've got to get out of here."

Dickie's "That's what I've been trying to tell you" response is a treasure. Buck escapes and gallops off with Dickie hot on his heels. Buck stops outside of town and sends Dickie back, but Dickie only pauses and follows once more.

Buck reaches the outlaws as they are preparing to board a small plane to fly to Mexico. Dickie arrives in time to film the whole thing.

Meanwhile, Drexel has been urged by his agent to go after Buck and the robbers to capture them. (It's never explained how somehow Grant suddenly has figured out how to ride a horse.) Drexel arrives, as the plane comes to a bumpy halt, and Buck discovers that Dickie followed him and was knocked winding by the action. Grant boasts about "his" capture of the bandits, while Buck is absorbed with getting Dickie to the hospital.

Buck tells Dickie that he must go back. As can be seen by the set of Dickie's jaw, no matter what Buck says, the youngster will be hot on his heels.

Carol blames Buck for taking Dickie with him and refuses to let Buck see the boy until all the hoopla has led to an award for bravery for Drexel.

When Dickie learns that Buck did try to see him and that Drexel is receiving acclaim for Buck's heroic deed, he sets out to set the record straight at the ceremony with the film he took of Buck lassoing the tail off the plane.

I liked Buck Jones a whole bunch, and he liked me, I guess, but in the first movie I did with him, they put that little dorky hat on me and he remembered that hat. So, when I came on the set in Hollywood Round-Up, *he said, "I've been looking for you. I got you a hat that looks like a hat."*

I had that hat for the longest time and don't know where I lost it. It was a real nice Stetson. He gave me my first pair of spurs, and I've worn them in every Western I've been in since.

Hollywood Round-up left some fine memories for Dick. Many of his films

Dick enjoys visiting with Buck Jones (center) and Lester Dorr during a break in the filming.

from that same time period he calls "just a job" and says nothing from them stands out, but he easily describes details of this one with Buck Jones.

I remember a few specifics about Hollywood Round-Up.

Helen Twelvetrees was a lovely lady—a nice lady.

There were about three Silvers. They train the horse to roll somebody along the ground—like Silver did me—with a barrel. Then, the person rolls instead of the barrel. He was a nice horse. He had a nice canter gait to him—didn't bounce you to pieces. He would stand still for trick mounts on him. He was a good horse. He was better than Champion, I think.

That little horse I rode in Hollywood Round-Up *I also rode in another picture. Nothing spectacular about him.*

The camera I had in that was a real camera. I had one like it, but I don't remember ever shooting anything I wanted to keep. It was a little 8mm—a real tiny film. You had about fifty, sixty feet of film.

In the scene when the horse is supposed to drag me, I threw a wide loop, and there were two or three guys standing out of camera range. I threw the rope out there and they took off running with it. You couldn't see the horse. The people who did this were part of the crew—grips.

Buck teaches Dickie some rope tricks just before Dickie ropes a horse and "forgets" to let go of the rope when the horse runs.

The old Columbia Ranch was the location for the street scene, which would be out at Thousand Oaks. The airstrip was the insert road up at upper Iverson's.

I know in one scene I had a white shirt on—a short-sleeve thing. Then, I had a satin shirt. I didn't have anything fancy like that when I was in Texas riding and roping. That satin shirt was made by Diamond, which is a fancy cowboy clothier. I've got a picture of me in that shirt and that hat sitting there posing.

I am too critical. I thought the last scene of Hollywood Round-Up *was awful damn corny.*

One of the films that Dick was not especially fond of was *Border Wolves*, starring Bob Baker as a singing cowboy. He had a nice voice, but the song placement brings some eye-rolling.

The last scene: Buck and Carol (Helen Twelvetrees) share a romantic moment while Dickie films it.

Rusty Reynolds (Bob Baker) and his pal, Clem Barrett (Fuzzy Knight), ride up immediately after an attack on a wagon train and are blamed for the attack. (The attack on the wagon train is footage from *Westward Ho*. That's Hank Bell, who is shot from the wagon seat and falls back into the wagon. Bell played Dick's dad in the John Wayne picture.)

Rusty is believed to be Jack Carson, a vicious outlaw, but Carson's father arranges their escape and sends Rusty to find his son and bring him back to him. They embark on a mission to hit the Hoot-Owl Trail in search of Jack Carson.

Along the way, Rusty stops a runaway coach with Mary Jo Benton (Constance Moore) on it. The horses ran away because Jimmie Benton (Dick Jones) hit one of the horses with his slingshot. He was aiming for the horse fly on the horse. It's not the only picture in which Dick's character causes problems with a slingshot.

Since they are heading the same direction, they ride on together, with Rusty singing in accompaniment to the rumble of the wheels. Jimmie joins in on his ukulele (small guitar?). It's a tribute to Dick's acting ability that he looks so enthusiastic about all the irrelevant songs that interrupt the action in *Border Wolves*.

Of course, Mary Jo, Jimmie, and their father live in the area that is now being terrorized by the Jack Carson gang. The marshal picks up Rusty, but Clem escapes and gets help from Ling Wong (Willie Fung), the Benton's cook.

As Marshal MacKay (Jack Montgomery) starts to take Rusty back, they meet Mary Jo and Jimmie, who tell them they will be on the stage the next day. The Carson gang plans to hold up that stage. Ling Wong helps Rusty escape, and he takes the marshal and his deputy to ride to the rescue.

As they ride along on the stage, Jimmie practices with his slingshot in case they are held up. When Mary Jo scorns the power of his slingshot, he replies, "Well, David knocked out Goliath, didn't he?"

Jimmie doesn't run off the gang, but when Rusty has been released by the lawmen and rushes to explain to Mary Jo, Jimmie uses his slingshot to propel Mary Jo into Rusty's arms.

Though Dick received fourth billing in *Border Wolves*, he doesn't have the screen time he does in a number of other films of this period.

He was blunt about his feelings for the film.

I think I liked Bob Baker's horse better than anything else. I wasn't a big fan of his. I didn't like that kind of cowboy singing and I didn't like people who would just bust into a song for no reason at all. I did enjoy working with Fuzzy Knight. We did a couple of days up in Lone Pine. The county fair was going on at that time and we'd go.

Dickie's lone Hopalong Cassidy film was *The Frontiersmen*, in which he played Artie Peters. Artie is a regular little demon—defying his aunt, putting burrs and stickers in beds and blankets, balking at taking a bath, talking back to adults, refusing to go to school then leading rebellion in the classroom when Hoppy coerces him into going. Hoppy is the only adult for whom he shows any respect.

Hoppy and the men are out trying to move the herd back from an area that is choice for rustling when the message comes that there's trouble in town at the schoolhouse. Hoppy leaves the cattle and dashes for town. With Hoppy gone the rustlers move in.

Artie's rabblerousing has gone to extremes but when Hoppy arrives the entire class is innocently singing with Artie conducting.

Artie (Dick Jones) catches sight of Hopalong Cassidy entering the schoolhouse as he directs the students in a song.

At last, the teacher makes enough noise from the closet where she is locked in, and Hoppy makes Artie let her out. She quits in a huff.

Hoppy decides he doesn't like the way the school is being run and goes to the state superintendent to ask for a new-style teacher. What he gets is June Lake (Evelyn Venable), who, of course, is young and beautiful.

Artie, along with every other male around, is smitten and going to school becomes very important to him. Now, he threatens the other kids if they give the teacher any trouble. The hands at the Bar 20 feel the same way and the school gets more screen time than the gang of rustlers plaguing the territory.

The Frontiersmen doesn't have a lot of action, despite the presence of some dependable Western stalwarts on both sides of the law. The Robert Mitchell Boy Choir, billed here as Robert Mitchell and his St. Brendan's Boys, make up the majority of the schoolchildren. They spend all their time singing rather than studying.

However, Dick has a good role in this one. He has a fun scene when he tries to get on his horse after Hoppy has spanked him and is too sore to get his foot up to the stirrup, so he then limps home leading his horse.

This film was another "it's a job" picture for Dick.

Hoppy didn't like me one little bit. We'd have dialog together and he never remembered his lines and I'd beat him to them. He didn't like that one little bit. I didn't pal around with him very much. I liked Russell Hayden, "Lucky"—nice guy.

Artie (Dick Jones), schoolteacher June Lake (Evelyn Venable), and Hopalong Cassidy (William Boyd) watch a rider come in from the porch of the Bar 20 ranch house.

The thing I remember most about that one was working with Evelyn Venable. I remember that real well because we came back from Big Bear location, and two days after we get home we're on the set at Disney Studio doing Pinocchio. *She was the Blue Fairy. She tweaked me with her magic wand and I became a real boy.*

Fifteen chapters of fast action make up *The Great Adventures of Wild Bill Hickok*, starring Wild Bill Elliott. Action comes so fast and furious that it is hard to predict the chapter breaks. Dick is seen all the way through, in several chapters being part of the cliffhanging chapter ending. This is a typical serial of the late 1930s but fun because of the number of Western "familiar faces" who dot the landscape. As Dick said, "You about had a who's who of Hollywood Westerns in that serial."

He wasn't kidding. In addition to Elliott and Monte Blue, Kermit Maynard played Kit Lawson, Roscoe Ates was Snake-Eyes, Reed Hadley portrayed Jim Blakely, who proposed to Ruth at the end, Chief Thundercloud was Chief Gray Eagle, J.P. McGowan played Scudder, and Eddy Waller was the vicious Stone. Uncredited roles were filled by such Western regulars as Hal Taliaferro (Wally Wales), Al Bridge, Bob Burns, Slim Whitaker, Blackjack Ward, Budd Buster, George Chesebro, Ed Cobb, Earl Dwire, Ernie Adams, Horace B. Carpenter, Hank Bell, Jack Montgomery, Tom London, Silver Tip Baker, Kenne Duncan, Earle Hodgins, Art Mix, Jack Rockwell, Ted Mapes, Artie Ortego, and Jack Perrin.

Chapters begin and end with a chorus shouting, "Wild Bill Hickok!" The action starts in Texas with a group of men led by Cameron (Monte Blue) organizing a trail drive to get their cattle to Abilene in order to get money to keep the carpetbaggers from taking their land. The carpetbaggers are already working to prevent that from happening.

The Phantom Raiders are organized. They are devoted to not only stopping the Texans from reaching Abilene but also to blocking the railroad from the town. They want no law and order or civilization anywhere.

Wild Bill Hickok has been appointed marshal to clean out the rotten element in Abilene and make sure that the cattle get though and so does the railroad. He rides into Abilene, shoots down three Raiders in a confrontation and proclaims, "I'm a peaceable man."

The leader of the Raiders offers a $5000 reward for the man who brings in Hickok's badge.

This serial was blessed with three dependable juvenile actors: Dick Jones as Buddy, the youngest of the three; Sammy McKim as Boots; and Frankie Darro as Jerry aka Little Brave Heart. Buddy is with the wagon train and cattle. Sammy is in Abilene. Jerry is living with the Indians. Even at their young ages, they could be called Western regulars, too.

Hickok has developed a society of boys called Flaming Arrows. They are dedicated to fight for the right. They support him and he comes to their aid. The secret password is "Our Country." It's not much of a secret as they shout it out in front of anyone and everyone.

It is never explained why a cattle drive on the Chisholm Trail includes a wagon train of women and children when the purpose of the drive is to save the land they have back home, but it does. It does make a nice opportunity for Buddy (Dick) and Cameron's daughter Ruth (Carole Wayne) to be endangered again and again at the end of chapters.

Ruth (Carole Wayne) holds Buddy's (Dick Jones) limp body after the ammunition wagon explosion leaves him stunned.

Dick remembered it this way:

I guess I was the cliffhanger on fourteen of the fifteen chapters. The one I remember the most was a runaway wagon filled with explosives and it goes over a cliff. I'm hanging out the back hollering, "Help! Help! Help!" and the announcer comes on, "Will Wild Bill Hickok be in time to save Buddy?" The next chapter comes along and he gets there just before the wagon goes over the cliff and explodes and he's got me and jerks me out of the wagon up onto his horse and we ride away into the sunset.

Actually, he wasn't the cliffhanger in that many of the chapters—Wild Bill himself was imperiled in some of them—but he was in danger often. It was almost always Buddy, Hickok or Ruth who might not survive.

Along the way, we learn that Jerry and Buddy have known each other in the past and are both Flaming Arrows. They are reunited when Jerry serves as a guide for a man from Abilene, who is hunting for Hickok with a message.

Jerry/Little Brave Heart (Frankie Darro) tries to protect Buddy (Dick Jones).

Later, when it appears that the wagons will be turning back rather than continuing to Abilene, Buddy runs away to find Jerry. One of the villains, a man who abused the two boys in the past, finds them and tries to capture them. Jerry dies saving Buddy and Dick has the opportunity to display his ability to cry on cue. He does a good job. Hickok finds Buddy crying over the body of his friend and vows to bring the killer to justice.

As Chapter Fourteen draws to an end, Buddy and Ruth have one last cliffhanging moment as the cattle are stampeded. Hickok rushes to save them as the final chapter opens.

Dick enjoyed working on Hickok.

I liked Gordon Elliott. I worked with him the first time in his first Western, Moonlight on the Prairie. *He was a dress extra, then played the sheriff in* Moonlight on the Prairie, *then turned around and was doing* The Great Adventures of Wild Bill Hickok. *That's the first time he put his guns on backwards.*

Wild Bill Hickok (Bill Elliott) talks with Buddy (Dick Jones) during a stop on the trail.

He was not a cowboy, per se, and not a horseman, per se, but he learned. He got on a horse and he had people instruct him and he turned out to be one of the best in the business. He liked being a cowboy. He was good.

We used up all of the Columbia's ranch photographical shots and they moved us up to Kanab. We were up at Kanab for a little over two weeks. We were all over Kanab. Went up to Kanab, RKO Ranch, Columbia Ranch. That was a long one—two or three weeks. That wasn't a show; it was a career.

Although Dick wasn't in the original serial, *The Lone Ranger* (1938), he can be seen in the condensation of it, *Hi-Yo Silver* (1940). *Hi-Yo Silver* is the feature-length cut of the 1938 serial, *The Lone Ranger*, with Lee Powell as the ranger and Chief Thundercloud as Tonto.

In order to bridge the gaps left from all the deleted footage, the film opens at the Lazy U Dude Ranch, where Smokey (Raymond Hatton) is brushing a big silver horse. The Boy (Dick Jones) comments that the horse is pretty. Smokey tells him the horse is the great-great grandson of the Lone Ranger's Silver. The boy asks, "Did you know the Lone Ranger?" When Smokey says yes, the boy (no name ever given) asks why he was called the Lone Ranger. "Tell me about it." Smokey tells him the story in a few scenes interspersed amongst archive footage from the serial.

Faithful *Range Rider* regular Stanley Andrews is the serial villain, though, of course, he and Dick had no scenes together. The achieve footage of Hank Bell being shot off the wagon seat—also used in two other films Dick was in, *Westward Ho* and *Border Wolves*—is retained from the serial in the feature-length version.

For those who want to see the highlights of the story without sitting through the length of the fifteen-chapter serial, it's a nicely abridged version.

Dick's comments:

I did the re-make [feature film version] of Hi-Yo Silver *– fifteen chapters. We did the segue between chapters and did it all in one day up at Lone Pine. Like the "tune in next week and see if the Lone Ranger can save Buddy from going over the cliff, or something like that." Instead of having a re-run of the last chapter, we would do that on the set and he would say, "Do you remember so-and-so and tell* him (me, the boy) the story of the Lone Ranger. And we did the segue between the middle of the fifteen chapters. They released it on the big screen as Hi-Yo Silver. With this you see the whole fifteen chapters of The Lone Ranger and it's barely an hour. There's less repeating of the previous chapter. Half a page of script catches you up—"meanwhile, back at the ranch."

Virginia City boasted a heavyweight cast: Errol Flynn, Randolph Scott, Humphrey Bogart, Alan Hale, Sr., Big Boy Williams, Miriam Hopkins, and Ward Bond in a minor role.

The plot was twisted and treacherous. Kerry Bradford (Errol Flynn), imprisoned in a Confederate prison camp, attempts escape with his buddies, Olaf Swenson (Alan Hale) and Marblehead (Big Boy Williams). The officer commanding the camp, Vance Irby (Randolph Scott), prevents the escape. Bradford vows to pay him back if the opportunity presents itself.

Julia Hayne (Miriam Hopkins), Irby's childhood friend and would-be lover, has been spying for the Confederacy in the West. She comes to Vance with the chance of financing for the Confederacy from Virginia City, Nevada. Irby sells the idea to Jefferson Davis and he leaves to organize the expedition.

Meanwhile, Bradford and his friends escape. Bradford had been working in intelligence and before being imprisoned he had determined that Virginia City is a likely source of gold for the Confederacy. They also head that way.

On the stage going West, the three, Julia, and a salesman find themselves sharing the ride with marauder John Murrell (Humphrey Bogart), who holds them up.

However, Bradford gets the drop on him and runs off Murrell's raiders, but in an action-packed sequence—achieved by master stuntman Yakima Canutt—Murrell escapes.

Julia begins to fall for Bradford, and he for her, setting up the conflict. She's driven to get the gold to the Confederacy. He's bound to stop it.

As the stage pulls into *Virginia City*, Cobby (Dick Jones) comes running to hook an arm on the stage and welcome Julia home. Bradford comments that he hopes all his rivals are so young.

Cobby is intricately involved in the effort to move gold to Richmond. He's the message runner and devoted to Miss Julia.

The Sazerac Saloon is the meeting place for all conspirators. That's where Bradford finds Julia—performing—and is shocked that she is "that kind of girl." He also spots Irby, and now knows who to watch to locate the gold for the Confederacy.

Bradford raids the blacksmith shop where the gold has been loaded into wagons but is too late. Olaf and Marblehead almost catch Irby at the doctor's where the doctor is patching up Murrell, who has come in with a bullet wound. Irby and Murrell make a deal and the plan to move the gold goes forward.

Dick does a fine job as Cobby, whose devotion to his friends and the cause lead to an early grave.

The Confederates take Bradford prisoner and take him with them as they start the long trek in the wagons.

When the wagons fail to pass inspection at a Union outpost, a gun battle ensues. Cobby falls from the wagon and is run over by a wheel.

Bradford escapes in the conflict but falls down a steep incline. His pursuers leave him for dead. Wrong. He crawls back to the outpost and telegraphs the Union army to pursue the wagon train.

Cobby needs rest to live but the wagons can't afford to stop. When Vance tells Cobby, he devotedly replies with understanding. And the wagons move on. The wagon movement worsens Cobby's injuries and he dies before they can make the next water source.

Dick did the action work himself.

That was one of my first good, big gags. When the horses got scared and reared up, I was jerked out of the wagon—that was me—I went down and had to land in a certain spot and the wagon was jerked forward and the camera was just far enough down to only get the hub of the wheel, and when I hit the dirt, two stuntmen were there to pull me out from under the wagon because the wagon went forward and rolled over a log that was there and the hub went up like it rolled over me and then they cut back to a different angle and there I was under the wagon.

Poor Cobby. He's dead. The director, Michael Curtiz, applauded me and said, "Very good. Very good. And for such a courageous act I award you this. A turquoise arrow." I remember Virginia City *well.*

Everything is against the wagon train. Water holes are dry. Bradford and the Union soldiers chase them. Murrell and his gang follow them to take the gold. It is truly a lost cause.

When Murrell's band attacks the wagon, Flynn and his friends ride in to help. Irby is wounded and Bradford takes over the defense efforts. Irby, aware that he is dying, tells Bradford where the gold is and Bradford takes steps to keep it from Murrell. He and his buddies bury the gold under a landslide.

The next morning, when Murrell's men attack the wagons, all seems to be lost until the troops Bradford sent for finally arrive. The Cavalry to the rescue.

Bradford is charged with treason for hiding the gold, and is court martialed. His execution is set for April 9, 1865. History majors will understand the significance of the day. Julia goes to Abraham Lincoln, who assures her Bradford will not be executed.

The experience of working in this film was a good one for Dick.

Virginia City *was made during the school break, so I didn't have to go to school, so I got to watch the filming. I got to sit behind the lights and watch.*

Errol Flynn, Big Boy Williams, and Alan Hale, Sr.—those three, when they weren't in front of the camera, were like teenage clowns. They were always pulling gags on each other.

I think Flynn topped them all. He got himself a standard-size schnauzer. Most people have miniatures. His was a big dog. He had it trained to heel about three or four feet behind him, not right on his heel. Most people have the dog heel right beside them. He always carried a swagger cane and would sling it around and he'd swagger with it. He'd slap his boot one time with that swagger stick and say "heel" and that dog would just fall in right behind him and follow along wherever Flynn went. When he'd stop, the dog would stop; when he'd move, he'd say heel, and the dog would go.

Then, he'd walk up to somebody and tap the stick on the other man's leg three times, and then he'd walk away and say heel, and the dog would come up and pee on the leg of the guy he tapped three times with the stick.

He'd chase Big Boy Williams around with that dog, and Big would say, "I'll kill him. I'll kill him if he slaps me with that swagger stick." It was fun watching them chase each other around.

I liked Flynn because of his humor and the way he worked with people. I think that's when I realized he was a real caballero. They used to talk about his after work orgies and stuff. I don't I pay any attention to that. It's what the guy does on the set and how he comes across and how he treats people. I got to know him real well on that set and liked him a lot.

Alan Hale was a good horsebacker. Big Boy Williams was better than any of them. He played professional polo.

What I remember of Randolph Scott—very prim, very personable. Randolph Scott was a real, real Southern gentleman, but he was very withdrawn, not outgoing, not gregarious. However, he would come on set, do his job, and go and wait for the next scene. If there was a follow-up, he wouldn't go back to his dressing room, he'd go over and sit down in his director's chair and out would come the Wall Street Journal. He perused the Wall Street Journal like it was The Bible. He'd do all these calculations between scenes. Always figuring, always calculating. Then, I guess, he had a runner to get him to do his investing for him. He sure was into that. He wasn't a party-goer; he didn't play cards; I don't ever remember him meeting with people after work to have a cocktail or anything like that. He was a nice guy. Easy to work with. All you'd have to do is be sure you had your lines down pat and he never missed a cue.

We worked at Warner Bros. indoors, then we went to Flagstaff, Arizona, and went down and worked in the Yuba desert. Yuba City, interesting location. Rolling desert. No bushes, no sagebrush, no cactus, no nothing—just sand.

Dick appeared in *Brigham Young, Frontiersman* in close proximity to *Virginia City*, but it left little impression. He remembered that the same young actress from *Destry Rides Again* played his sister, and he shared a thought on Jane Darwell.

I worked with Jane Darwell several times. I remember her most as the matriarch in Brigham Young. *She was our mother or head of the clan. She was a grand old lady—very professional.*

You don't work that much and not be. They talk about these prima donnas that think that they are the greatest and the stuff they pull—be late on the set and never know their lines. You didn't really work often if you were down the line and off the "star" list. If you weren't professional, you wouldn't get a callback.

The film is titled *Brigham Young,* and Dean Jagger was the title character, but the stars were Tyrone Power and Linda Darnell. Reviews of this biopic were lukewarm at best. Power played Jonathan Kent. Dick was Henry Kent, and Ann Todd played his sister, Mary. Dick made no comments on the film's stars.

Dick had only a small role in the infamous tale of Billy the Kid, *The Outlaw*. He is the leader of a group of kids who are debating whether Billy the Kid is really Billy the Kid. The Kid (Jack Buetel) walks out and they pepper him with questions. Dick (nameless character here) has a piece of wood he wants to make into a whistle. Billy the Kid shoots it hollow for him with Dick holding it. Dick thanks him and the kids run off. End of Dick's role in *The Outlaw*.

It's All a Blank

IN HIS EARLY YEARS, DICKIE PLAYED a number of roles that left no lasting impression on him. It's easy to understand that a five-to-eight-year-old child, whose part was a boy of his age who was just one of a family, might not recall each and every performance.

In the first place, acting was not his shining goal. He didn't want to be a "shimmering star on screen" but an ordinary kid. He expressed that to me any number of times, as I quizzed him about his character or the actors with whom he shared screen time.

Some of those films are unavailable on DVD or video, ones whose popularity faded by the time they had finished their theater runs around the country. When Dick finally agreed to share some of his experiences, I began searching for videos of every movie in the filmography he provided me. A number of them, I never found. Discussions of these films will be brief, basically a note about the plotline, the lead performers and that Dick appeared in them.

Let's start with one that he knew he was in, but remembered not at all, *Exclusive Story*. In it, newspaperman Tim Higgins (Stuart Erwin) looks for chance to bring a crime boss to justice. Dick has a couple of scenes as the newsman's older son. It's a melodramatic and anguish-filled tale, typical of one style of mid-thirties crime drama.

Dick did have a couple of nice lines in the scene when Higgins is playing battle with his sons in the living room. The scene is short, interrupted by a phone call that sends the dad back to work.

Dick is at the bottom of the pile in the copy of the worn still he gave me. That's Jane Darwell commanding, obviously the mother-in-law.

Another forgettable film was *The First Baby*.

Videos or DVDs for home viewing of this one were nonexistent from every source I tried. Dick had a copy of a still showing him in this movie, but other than plot descriptions from film history sources and the lead players, it is not a noted film. It is a story of mother-in-law interference when a young couple has a baby.

One film Dick did not include in his filmography was *Sutter's Gold*. The mostly fictional biography of Johan Sutter, on whose property gold was discovered in California, was a box office disaster. Dick had a few minutes in the last five minutes of the film. He was one of three newspaper boys who played a joke on Sutter when he was in Washington, D.C. It is a forgettable role in a forgettable movie.

Edgar Kennedy, master of the slow burn, made a popular series of shorts for RKO. Dick was in one of these, *Gasoloons*, and in another short of the same vintage, *Who's Looney Now*. Dick remembered very little about them, when asked about the experience.

"I remember working in them and I've seen them, but I don't remember much except Edgar Kennedy."

Despite two scenes critical to the story of *Girls on Probation*, Dick had limited screen time and it made little impression on him.

Jane Bryan was the innocent dupe, and Ronald Reagan the honest man who believed in her.

Connie Heath (Jane Bryan) is not too bright when it comes to picking friends. Her "good" friend, Hilda Engstrom (Sheila Bromley), doesn't have a good bone in her body. She steals, she lies, she leads Connie right into jail, but Connie keeps defending her until Hilda runs away, leaving Connie charged with larceny.

When Connie discovers Hilda in another city and confronts her as they sit in a car in front of a bank, Dick, who sells magazines on that corner, hears the argument—just before Hilda's confederate runs from the bank, money in hand, and refuses to let Connie escape from the car as they drive away.

Though Dick has only a handful of lines and a few scenes in *Girls on Probation*, his role is pivotal and he plays it well. Without his ever-so-convincing testimony, poor Connie would have been doing one-to-five.

Twice more in the same time period, Dickie had important roles in films that left him with no stories to tell and few memories, *Black Legion* and *Flying Fists*.

Black Legion is a story of an angry man, Frank Taylor (Humphrey Bogart) wooed by men who use his irrational ire to seduce him into joining a terror organization. Those sucked into the Black Legion think they are partnering with men like themselves to present a united front but actually they are lining the pockets of a group of shysters who only want their money.

Dick plays Frank's son Buddy, Erin O'Brien-Moore, his wife Ruth, and Dick Foran, his pal Ed from work on whom he finally turns.

Nothing stood out in Dick's mind from this film and it is easy to see why. His role is that of a loving, trusting son. No line is other than a child might say in a family setting, nor does any of the violence of the film involve him.

One of young Dickie's greatest talents was naturally being a child. In this, and other roles as a child in the family, he delivers lines so naturally one would think that he was adlibbing exactly what *he* would say under those circumstances. There's nothing stiff or set-up feeling about his presence, and that very gift may have caused some to underrate his immensely capable acting.

Flying Fists may have been a B-film, but Dick had a stand-out role in it. It is still another of his 1930s films in which his role was pivotal to the story.

Hal Donovan (Bruce Bennett as Herman Brix) is a lumberjack, minding his own business, when he is confronted by former boxing contender Slug Cassidy (Guinn "Big Boy" Williams) over some flying chips. He knocks Slug cold, and Slug and his manager, Spider (Fuzzy Knight), convince Hal to join the fight game.

His billing as "Chopper," who hates everyone, is a direct contrast with his nature. He meets Kay Conrad (Jeanne Martel), who hates boxing because her father was once a fighter and the game ruined his health. Before Hal has time to change her mind, Slug and Spider anonymously mail her some of Hal's press clippings. (It is interesting casting that both Guinn "Boy Big" Williams and Fuzzy Knight are the villains of the piece in this film. For most of their careers both played chiefly comic relief roles.)

Kay turns on him and Hal turns on Slug and Spider, walking out on them and going to California to work at a health camp run by another former fighter, Bill "One Punch" Fagin (J. Farrell MacDonald). It just so happens that Kay and her father have gone to the same town for her father's treatment.

In this little town, Hal "Smith" is known as an all-right guy and is the idol of the local kids, including Dickie Martin (Dick Jones). He teaches them to be upright and honest and inspires Dickie to tell the truth about a prank rather than lie to get away with it.

Hal and Kay discover each other, with a little help from their dogs, and get together again.

Dickie takes dance lessons from Kay. At a group practice of the waltz, he tells her he doesn't want to dance but to be a boxer, to which she replies that any successful boxer must have great footwork. In a fun scene, Dick demonstrates his own footwork in a rousing tap dance. It is a must-see for his fans.

Slug and Spider bring their new contender to town on a tour to take on local favorites for three rounds to promote their new hopeful.

The locals assure the promoters that Smith is the man to represent them. When he goes in for his interview, he discovers who is running the show and finds they want him to take a dive. He walks out on them again.

Then, the doctor tells Kay that her father must have surgery that they can't afford. Hal, compelled by the desire to save the life of Kay's father, goes back to the unscrupulous promoters and makes the deal.

Hal feels bad enough, but when Dickie tearfully confronts him about the rumor he has heard about the fight, Hal cannot respond to the boy's say-it-isn't-so pleas. It's another fine scene for Dick.

Dickie goes to Kay and tells her and her father what has transpired. Her father says he'd rather die than be saved that way, and sends Kay and Dickie to tell Hal that he must fight to win.

Monk (William "Billy" Benedict) goes to confront Hal Smith (Bruce Bennett as Herman Brix) along with Dickie Martin (Dick Jones) when they hear that he plans to take a dive and lose the fight.

Dickie (Dick Jones, second from right) and Kay (Jeanne Martel, right) plead with Bruce Bennett (right) to fight honestly as Bill "One Punch" Fagin (J. Farrell MacDonald) listens.

They convince Hal to make it a fair fight and he tells Slug and Spider the deal is off. With Kay and Dickie cheering him on, he goes into the ring.

Flying Fists is a movie that shows off Dick's considerable performance skills. He boasts, he dances, he pleas, he cries, and his facial and physical reactions to the fight are dead on. He even gets to tussle with Billy Benedict for some footage before Bruce Bennett breaks up the fight.

Though the script is on the corny side and production values are definitely B, this was a good film for Dick and a fun one for his fans.

One might say that *Love Is on the Air* left Dick speechless. The most he said was, "It was a job." In it, Ronald Reagan plays a radio reporter fighting crime.

Another "it's a blank" of that time was *Devil's Party*. In this one Dickie grows up to be John Gallaudet, ambitious policeman Joe O'Mara, in a drama about childhood friends growing up to find themselves in conflicting circumstances. Victor McLaglen was the star of this B-quality, but intriguing, tragedy.

Several times, Dick was shown or given a copy of a movie he was in that he didn't know about. One of these was *Beware Spooks!*

There's one I didn't even know about. It was a Joe E. Brown movie. I had a hell of a good part in that thing with three other kids. I only got to see it quickly—just my part that Boyd [Magers] showed me, so I don't know too much about it. It was called Beware Spooks! *I didn't even have it on my list of things that I did. He said, "You were in that one." Then, he comes up with the tape and, "There you are."*

Beware Spooks! is typical Joe E. Brown farce. Roy Gifford (Brown) is a bumbling policeman trying to be reinstated after being fired. Coincidentally, he and his bride (Mary Carlisle) honeymoon right by the Spook House used by the crooks for their connecting place.

Dick's role in *Beware Spooks!* takes place outside the spook house. Gifford's bride leaves a trail of saltwater taffy for him to follow as she follows baddie Danny Emmett (George J. Lewis) down the row of carnival hawkers to the spook house. Gifford picks up the pieces of taffy as he trails her but comes abruptly face-to-face with Dick and Tommy Bupp, who are picking up the candy from the other end of the trail. When a cop appears, Gifford hands all the candy he has picked up to the boys.

It's no wonder this role slipped Dick's mind.

Interestingly enough, George J. Lewis, who would play an assortment of villains and good guys in *The Range Rider* and *Buffalo Bill, Jr.* series, is the second ranked bad man behind Marc Lawrence in this film. He and Dick had no scenes together at this time, but had many together later.

Sergeant Madden, in which he played the only child in the Madden household who was not adopted, was a blank in Dick's mind. Dickie portrays young Dennis Madden, who is labeled the rebellious child of the family. He had the skill to create the background for the adult Dennis (Alan Curtis) to cross ideas with his father all the way.

Dick explains the lack of remembrance of working with Wallace Beery and other adult actors this way:

At that age, I had to go to school. I had to have three hours of school, an hour for recreation, an hour for lunch. That doesn't give you much time to work. The social worker keeps me out of the way and off the set. You're a kid and the actors don't have time for you, so you don't get to mingle with the adults.

In *Sky Patrol*, "Tailspin Tommy" Tompkins (John Trent) and his buddy, "Skeeter" (Milburn Stone), are training a Reserve Corps of Army pilots to watch the coast for smugglers. Colonel Meade's (Boyd Irwin) son, Carter (Jackie Coogan), is a recent graduate, but he wants to be a doctor and save lives, not be a fighter.

Nevertheless, he goes out on patrol and spots an amphibian plane where one should not be. It is the smugglers. They shoot down his plane and, when they realize who he is, they capture him rather than kill him then.

Tommy and Skeeter throw out a full search for the amphibian. They field many false leads before a report comes in that a "twelve-year-old boy" has called in a sighting of the amphibian plane the Sky Patrol is seeking. Tommy and Skeeter hop into a car and go out to investigate.

There, as if waiting for them to arrive, in the front yard of a house, working on a model airplane is Bobby Landers (Dick Jones). Yes, he saw the amphibian. Yes, he knows one plane from another. He and a friend have been logging flights. This particular aircraft has been illusive, so he is proud to finally get the number. And, yes, he can tell them which direction the airplane went. He goes with them to locate the warehouse being used for a landing base, and Tommy promises him a ride in a plane, but that's the last we see of Dick in this picture.

I Remember...

SOME OF THE FILMS of Dick's early years provided him with a memorable moment or two.

The Kid Comes Back, with Wayne Morris, Barton MacLane and June Travis, left no mass of vivid stories Dick loved to tell, but he did make a comment.

The Kid Comes Back was with Wayne Morris. I remember Slapsie Maxie Rosenbloom. He was fun to work with. He talked just like he was a beat-up boxer like he was really. It was typecasting.

Long time ago. Night shot at Warner Bros.

Dick's role was key to a turn in the story when Rosenbloom cheats the young newsboy Bobby (Dick Jones). But when pressed, Dick had nothing else to say about the movie. It is a typical boxing story of the time period.

What Dick remembered from *The Man Who Dared* and his attitude toward it is a real head-shaker for most people. The more adventurous the activity required of him, the more "interesting" he found it. Part of that was undoubtedly from a young boy's point of view. What was "interesting" to me was the risk factor in what he was allowed to do.

He commented:

The Man Who Dared. Charlie Grapewin. I remember that somehow I got kidnapped or I got in the way of the gangsters and they wrapped me up in a blanket and threw me down on the floor. When the cops came in and raided the place, they shot the hell out of the room with a Thompson submachine gun, and I remember they put up boards—two-by-sixes or something like that—on the inside of the door big enough to cover me—a silhouette—and then they shot holes in the door. That was before they came up with the squibs that they could set off electronically, and they had a guy actually shoot the machine gun. To get the realization of me lying there getting shot at, they had all those holes tracing my outline in the door. I thought it was very interesting—not scary. I didn't know any different.

This crime drama of town corruption is difficult to find for viewing. It is one of the films I wanted to see before putting this book together, but was not able to locate a purchasable copy. Dick did not have a personal copy.

A Man to Remember was one of the "lost" RKO movies of the 1930s, reshown in recent years after a lengthy time of unavailability. It is the story of John Abbott (Edward Ellis), a small town doctor, whose life's work is helping those others have turned away. While other doctors in town put money first, Doc Abbott takes his pay in pigs, eggs, and corn.

The doctor is a widower raising a son. Soon after moving to Westport, he is also raising a "daughter," the child of a man who abandons her when the mother dies in childbirth.

Young Dick Abbott is played by Dick Jones, who grows up to be Lee Bowman. It was usually in the B-movies that Dick's screen name was the

John Abbott (Edward Ellis) and his son, Dick (Dick Jones), welcome the new baby who will become Dick's sister.

same as his own, but in *A Man to Remember,* Dick plays Dick. His role is one of a number in which he plays a typical member of a family. Though he is very good in it, there was little involved to make it stand out in his memory.

As a youngster, Dick Abbott is a good boy, but he grows up to favor the financial benefits of practicing medicine more than adhering to the principles of his father. It takes a polio epidemic to make him see the light.

The film was well-received by critics in 1938, but in making the moral point, it goes almost into overkill. The good doctor seems to be the only man in town who puts a concern for humans over the desire for money. Store owner Ramsey (Harlan Briggs) is much more concerned about the cost of the operation than whether or not his wife will live.

It's another of the films in which Dick does a good job, yet all his fans may not find the film to their taste.

Dick was casual about it.

I remember working in it. I remember seeing it. I remember Anne Shirley was supposed to be my sister when she grew up. The copy I saw came from The Netherlands and had Dutch subtitles. They didn't take them off when they showed it on Turner Classic Movies.

Dickie worked with Sybil Jason in *Woman Doctor*, starring Frieda Inescort. When asked about the film, he said:

Sybil Jason. As much as we were working, we only worked that one picture together. The only thing I remember about that is the scene where I'm supposed to be crippled from infantile paralysis and I'm doing the exercises. But I remember Sybil Jason because we went to school together on the set. She lives up here about a mile and a half from me. I see her at the post office all the time.

Young Mister Lincoln was just another job for Dick.

I only worked with John Ford once, on Young Mister Lincoln. *I was in the covered wagon and I didn't have a lot to say.* [Actually, he had no lines.]

All I remember of Young Mister Lincoln *is riding in a wagon and having to get some books out of the wagon. Henry Fonda said, "I want those books. I want those books.*

Fluffy, fun, and not to be taken seriously, *Nancy Drew . . . Reporter* starred Bonita Granville and Frankie Thomas, Jr. as Nancy Drew and Ted Nickerson, changed from the *Ned* Nickerson of the books. Ted's younger sister, Mary (Mary Lee), and her pal Killer Parkins (Dick Jones) live to annoy her brother and Nancy. Whatever strategies they can come up with, they put into action.

They make their entry with car whistle bombs. Nancy thinks they are trying to blow up her car but they just want to laugh.

Dick had a lengthy story about the whistle bombs that showed a sense of humor some may have missed.

I glommed onto a couple of dozen of those car whistle bombs and I played with them over the years up until maybe the 1950s—I got so many of them.

We used them in Nancy Drew . . . Reporter, *played a gag on somebody and got chastised for that. I kept them and I had fun with them.*

I put them on some friends' cars when they were least expected. One of them I remember very well. A friend of mine was getting married. I got there and jacked

I Remember...

Nancy Drew (Bonita Granville) restrains Killer Parkins (Dick Jones) and Mary Nickerson (Mary Lee) after they plant whistle bombs in her car, as Ted Nickerson (Frankie Thomas, Jr.) watches.

up the differential of the back of his car just enough so the wheels would spin, but they wouldn't get traction, and I hooked up one of those things under the hood so that when they turned the ignition to get the car started the bomb went off. It starts off with a whistle and the smoke comes out and then it goes "Boom." They were halfway down the next block when they thing exploded. Then, when they came back, they couldn't get his car to run. The engine would go and the wheels would spin, but they wouldn't go anywhere until he, when getting out, knocked it off the jack and it started going down the road without him in it. His bride's standing over on the side just cussing me. "I'll kill you if I ever catch you." I thought it was funny.

The next time the kids show up, they are in the rumble seat of Nancy's car, annoying Ted. When asked about the rumble seat, Dick said:

The rumble seat didn't make an impression because that was a normal thing back in those days. Betty's [Jones] brother had a '31 Ford coupe with a rumble seat, and whenever he had to haul other kids they'd all end up in the rumble seat. Most girls didn't like them because there was no protection from the wind and they'd get their hair all messed up. They tied bandannas around their hair trying to keep it in place, from blowing like witches wings.

Killer and Mary stow away when Nancy and Ted go to a Chinese restaurant to spy on the murderer and the girlfriend of his henchman. Mary threatens to call Nancy's father if they aren't allowed to go in with her and Ted, and they order more than anyone in the group has enough money to cover.

Nancy calls the henchman and instigates a brawl in the restaurant, then all four juveniles are headed for a pile of dirty dishes in the kitchen in order to work off the bill they can't pay until Killer suggests they sing for their supper. This becomes a "don't miss" film for Dick Jones fans when the kids perform a medley of nursery rhyme songs. While Dick can be seen dancing on screen a number of times, this is one of his few singing scenes.

Killer Parkins (Dick Jones), Mary Nickerson (Mary Lee), Ted Nickerson (Frankie Thomas, Jr.), and Nancy Drew (Bonita Granville) perform to pay for their food.

One of Dick's bits in this movie is talking like Donald Duck, something he did very effectively, that is featured in this musical number.

I don't really remember the nursery rhyme song lyrics. I just remember we danced and I did the juvenile jive all over the place. Mary Lee died too young. She was just a couple of years older than me because she had to go to school, too.

I could do that Donald Duck imitation real well. They say that I was more understandable than Clarence Nash [the voice of Donald Duck at that time] *was. I was doing it all the time on the Disney set.*

At the end of the show, the little pranksters are back to whistle bombs.

During our talk on this film--one of my favorites of his juvenile roles and also one of his wife's favorites—I asked him about some specifics.

He told me:

I was a little kid. Most adults don't like to mess around, play around, or pal around with little kids. So, I really didn't get any social time with the adults. And I imagine at that time Frankie Thomas said, "Get away from me, kid. I can't be bothered."

They filmed the fight when I was in school. Remember, when I wasn't working, the social worker would come grab me by the ear and sit me down and make me do my lessons.

Mr. Stewart

DICK THOUGHT VERY HIGHLY OF JAMES STEWART and appeared in three films with him. From the first one, when he was quite young, the player who left the outstanding imprint on his memory was not Stewart but Jean Harlow.

Wife vs. Secretary held a cast of notables. Van (Clark Gable) and Linda (Myrna Loy) Stanhope have a wonderful marriage. Linda knows her husband loves her and has no feelings of jealousy for Van's gorgeous and very efficient secretary Whitey (Jean Harlow). Unfortunately, all the women in Linda's life take one glance at Whitey and start whispering smutty suggestions in her ear—even Van's mother.

Circumstances twist to give Linda hints of what could be inappropriate behavior, but both Van and Whitey are innocent of illicit intentions, and, at last, it all turns out for the best in the end.

James Stewart is Whitey's boyfriend Dave, hoping to become a fiancé. When he joins the family dinner table, Dick is plainly seen in his non-speaking role as Whitey's little brother, drinking his glass of milk.

Harlow made a memorable impression on young Dickie.

I was just a kid in the family. One scene in particular where Jean Harlow was there. What a sex pot she was! That's the thinking of a six-year-old.

Jean Harlow was a beautiful lady. I think I was growing up because I noticed it. That's the first time I worked with Jimmy Stewart. Jimmy and I talked about that when we worked on Mister Smith Goes to Washington. *Way back then with Jean Harlow. He remembered Jean Harlow, also.*

Destry Rides Again was James Stewart's first Western and a popular film of its time. Among other memorable scenes, the cat fight between Marlene Dietrich and Una Merkel in the saloon is one of the most remembered female fights in film history.

The story takes place in the town of Bottleneck, which is controlled by Kent (Brian Donlevy) and his cronies. When he steals Lem Claggett's (Tom Fadden) ranch in a crooked poker game, the sheriff has barely started to asked questions before he "disappears." The mayor promptly appoints the town drunk, Washington Dimsdale (Charles Winninger), the new sheriff. Dimsdale calls for help—the son of the famous lawman Wash once served as deputy, Tom Destry (Stewart). The problem is that Young Destry has traded his guns for a law book.

At the sheriff's office, Eli Whitney Claggett (Dick Jones) meets Thomas Jefferson Destry when his mother sends him for the sheriff, and the boy is impressed to meet someone of his reputation. Kent, backed by his henchmen, is demanding possession of the ranch at gunpoint. When Destry hears the facts and sees the IOU Claggett signed, he agrees that the Claggetts must leave the property. Dick's non-verbal demonstration of admiration-changed-to-disgust is true to life and on target.

This scene was vague in Dick's memory.

I know mother sends me to get the sheriff. I remember a group of us in the living room. She [Virginia Brissac] *came to me and said you gotta go. There was an old guy* [Tom Fadden], *who was supposed to be the father, and the woman was the mother, and Ann Todd as the little girl. She was the cutest little girl and a darned good little actress. She was my sister in* Brigham Young *that we did up in Lone Pine, also. I don't know whatever became of her. The trouble with girls is when they grow up and get married they change their name and then they get lost. She was no relation to the actress Ann Todd, and I have no idea how they could have the same name in the Screen Actors Guild.*

I worked with George Marshall [the director] *several times. He was a real good director. I had no problems with him.*

Wash wants Tom to just go back where he came from, but Tom has other ideas in mind. He wants to see Kent and his cohorts punished and the Claggetts get their ranch back, but not accomplished with a six-gun.

He moves things along in his slow, careful way until the villains shoot Wash, then he puts on the guns he took off and goes after Kent.

One of the notable scenes is when the men start out with guns, Frenchy (Marlene Dietrich) organizes the women to stop the gunplay. Their mob march down the street and into the saloon is both effective in reaching the goal of running out the bad men and entertaining for the audience.

Most people remember Dick in *Destry Rides Again* for the final scene as he walks with Stewart, mimicking his every move and word. That piece of cinema is a treasure, infinitely watchable over and over.

Dick remembered *Destry Rides Again* fondly, especially his relationship with James Stewart.

My memory of Destry *was palling around—if you want to call it that—the relationship with Jimmy Stewart. He treated me not like a little bitty kid to be shut up and stuck in a corner but like an adult. We'd go over scenes together and he'd explain things to me, and when we were working that walking down the street scene, he said, "Just watch me and do what I'm doing." He was real nice. I walked down the street copy-catting him.*

After that, we did Mister Smith Goes to Washington, *so I got a real good camaraderie with him. We'd always say hi, call each other by name. I'd call him Mr. Stewart; he'd call me Dickie or Richard at church.*

I wish I had a still of that last scene where I'm dressed up like Jimmy Stewart and walking down the street. We're both whittling and I'm trying to emulate him. I would love to have a still of that one, but this friend of mine who can make a still off videos couldn't get a good still out of it.

A fun bit to watch for in the film is Destry's illustrating points by telling a story. All start, "I knew a man . . . ." or "I had a friend . . . ." until he is told he knows too many men. Another is his business of constantly tucking in the front of Wash's shirt, which is always hanging over the front of his pants. After Boris/Callahan (Misha Auer) joins Wash and Tom in the sheriff's crew, he tucks in the sheriff's shirt, too.

Frank Capra's *Mister Smith Goes to Washington* was an important film of 1939. With James Stewart in the title role and a cast loaded with seasoned talent, it has remained a classic over the years.

To recap the story briefly: Senator Sam Foley dies before an important bill is due to come to the floor. Political boss Jim Taylor (Edward Arnold) tells the governor that he will appoint a particular crooked politician, but the reaction is so violent that the governor hesitates. At dinner, the governor's sons tell him he should appoint the man who has done so much for the boys of the state, Jefferson Smith.

It sounds like a good way out of the dilemma. This Smith fellow won't be savvy enough to cause any damage. His father and the other senator from the state, Joseph Paine (Claude Rains), were friends and Paine can sway him to go along.

To the dismay of the politicians, Smith is naïve, honest, honorable, and determined to make a difference for the people he serves. The film is a familiar one, and no spoilers will be here for those who are not already reminiscing as they read.

Dick played the pageboy, who shows Smith to his seat when he first arrives on the Senate floor. He tells him the desk he has was once used by

Daniel Webster. Smith is far more impressed than others who have heard those words. Dick gives him a visual tour of the Senate, pointing out the visitors' gallery, reporters' area, and other specified locations. When Dick is preparing to leave Smith, the new Senator asks him his name. Dick's reply, "Richard Jones," is the only credit he received on this film.

Despite the lack of credit and minimal screen time, this film stood out in Dick's memory.

Frank Capra was a very quiet, very astute director. He was an artist. He would paint a picture in his mind of what he wanted and then he would stick with it until he got it on film. He would work with me. As far as I was concerned, he wouldn't scream or holler at me or anything like that.

The other thing I remember, other than the director, was I didn't get billing in that show. It was verbal. They used my name when Jimmy Stewart says, "And who are you?" And I said, "I'm Richard Jones." And he said, "Okay, Dick. Thanks for showing me around." I got verbal; I didn't have anything on the screen.

Dick commented on fellow actors.

Another funny thing about Mister Smith Goes to Washington, *Jean Arthur is the only female actress I ever worked with that I ever asked for an autograph. She impressed me that much. She really knocked my socks off because she came back with an 11x14 matted sepia-toned picture of her in a formal, white evening gown—a real cheesecake-type picture—signed "To Dickie, with love, Jean Arthur." I've got that hanging in my den. She wasn't my very favorite, but I liked her a lot.*

Claude Rains? Good actor.

I knew Harry Carey, Sr. long before Mister Smith Goes to Washington. *I liked the part he played in* Angel and the Badman. *He played the sheriff. That's the way I remember him.*

Mister Smith Goes to Washington was a standout film for Dick. He found opportunity to revisit the venue in later years.

My daughter takes school groups on a trip to Washington, D.C. She's been doing it so long she's got all the connections to get into different chambers.

I said, "Gee, I'd sure like to go with you sometime."

"You couldn't keep up with me," she said.

I said, "Don't bet on that."

She said, "I've got a better idea."

So, when they had us up there to Williamsburg [Film Festival], *the first time they gave me the opportunity that if I wanted to sightsee to come a couple of days early or stay over. I don't stay over. When it's over, I've got to get out of there. So, I said, "I'll come early."*

When we got to Williamsburg, my daughter rented a car and we drove up to Washington, D.C., and got a hotel up there and had two days of just going all over Washington, D.C.

When we went to the Capitol, she had several of the Senators lined up to talk to. The chaplain at the Senate used to be the pastor at our Hollywood First Presbyterian Church that we all liked. We went to see him and then we went into the Senate. We approached it from the balcony and I'm looking down on it. In my eyes, I saw the same carpeting they were using on the Senate floor when we did Mister Smith Goes to Washington. *I come up to the rail and I say, "That's the same damn carpeting they had in* Mister Smith Goes to Washington.*"*

He said, "Well, we're not spending money like people think we do."

"Little Wooden Head"

WALT DISNEY'S 1940 FILM CLASSIC, *Pinocchio*, is considered by many to be the pinnacle of Disney animation. The richness and beauty of the art is the work of masters. Even today, most people have seen it in childhood or as adults watching with their children or grandchildren.

Dick Jones had the chance to provide the voice of Pinocchio in an interesting way.

Dick had a role in the classic Barbara Stanwyck tearjerker, *Stella Dallas*. He plays Lee Morrison, son of Helen Morrison (Barbara O'Neil), the woman Stephen Dallas (John Boles) marries after he and Stella (Barbara Stanwyck) break up.

He also reprised this role on radio on the *Lux Radio Theatre*.

In Dick's own words:

I did Lux Radio Theatre. *It was* Stella Dallas *with Barbara Stanwyck.* Lux Radio *did a radio version of the movie. That's how I got in it because I was one of the sons.*

And because I was on radio—or so they thought—I was on the cast call to audition for Pinocchio. *They only wanted people with radio experience. And of course I had all kinds of experience—or they thought I did.*

I got the part of Pinocchio through auditions—interviews and voice tests. Disney gave the direction to stop using adults to imitate child's voices. He wanted the real little boy's voice. The adults came close, but it sounded like Betty Boop. They got all the kids that had radio experience, that had Guild cards, that had worked, that could read the script, and they interviewed and tested all of them. After about 200 kids tested for that, it whittled down to the two of us—Sammy McKim and me—and we were very good friends. And we still ended up friends because I got the role of Pinocchio and he got a lifetime job at Disney. He was an artist. They hired him as an artist. He did the map of Disneyland.

After maybe a month back and forth, back and forth, I got a call that Mr. Disney wanted to have lunch with my mother and me at the cafeteria at the old Hyperion Studio. Well, being invited to lunch only meant one thing—that he had decided on me for the part. I went with all expectations of being told "you're the winner," that sort of thing, so he said very calmly, "Dickie, how would you like to have the part of Pinocchio?" And I thought, what the hell do you think I've been doing all this stuff for? But I didn't say that. I jumped up and clapped and said, "Oh goodie, goodie. That's the most important thing I want to do." I acted like I was very thrilled—which I was—but I had to show it not just say it. So, he said, "Well, you've got the part," and I started to work with it. That's all there was to that.

Pinocchio was the work of years. The Disney crew adapted the original story to make it more palatable to modern audiences. The original book, *The Adventures of Pinocchio* by Carlo Collodi, was a product of the 1880s and harsh for American moviegoers of 1940. In the book, Pinocchio was a truly bad boy, more akin to the Lampwick character in the Disney version than

Disney's Pinocchio character. He smashes the cricket who tries to be his conscience and is hanged at the hands of the fox and the cat. (Can you say Honest John and Gideon?)

Though the Disney version is lighter, it still has its dark moments. The concept of looking into a mirror and seeing a donkey as Lampwick does is pure horror. And Monstro the Whale has created many a nightmare for young theatergoers.

The innocence of the Disney Pinocchio character wins over the darkness. With his features more rounded rather than the lanky, angular build of the earlier illustrations, and the little boy lilt of young Dickie's voice, this version of *Pinocchio* never fails to charm. Add Jiminy Cricket, voiced by the versatile Cliff "Ukulele Ike" Edwards, plus the full cast of qualified actors to vocalize the masterfully animated characters, and the film is a winner.

Dick enjoyed remembering the months that he worked on *Pinocchio*.

I was on it nineteen months, but they worked on it a lot longer than that. They took all the animation, sound, and all. They had to do to do frame by frame drawings. They had to take each frame. It took a couple of years.

I had the best contract ever—of any show. They worked me at my leisure. I did six other movies while I did Pinocchio. *They'd say we have a scene we want to do, when can you come in, and I'd look at my schedule—or my mother would—and if I was working another show, she'd say we can be there at such and such and they'd arrange that scene at my leisure. So, I had a real good contract. I finished when I was eleven.*

The way they do it now, it they get the scenes ready and the actors put the voice with the animation. We didn't have a completed script. We would do scene by scene. It would be like looking at large funny papers—comics. They'd take a storyboard and they'd pin up the drawings of perceived action and they'd give us a script for that one scene.

Today, you go into a sound room by yourself and look at what you're supposed to lip sync and do it all by yourself. I don't know how you can get the feeling of what's going on if other actors aren't there so you can get their reaction. I worked with Jiminy Cricket. We worked face to face across an easel with a script. I worked the same way with Evelyn Venable, the Blue Fairy. I worked very closely with Christian Rub, who was Gepetto. Walter Catlett was Honest John/J. Worthington Foulfellow. He was a lot of fun to work with. His cohort, the little cat, was done by Mel Blanc. Only one line—one hiccup. I never worked with Gideon.

I never did a scene by myself. There was always someone else working with me. We all worked with each other. I don't know how they do it today and make it believable. Of course, it's not believable to me. Computer animation is flat. Doesn't have any life to it.

Everybody that worked on Pinocchio *showed their love for the show. That's why it turned out to be a classic. It's still pretty good for seventy years.*

Walt Disney was very hands-on in the films he made. He was the boss. But he never stepped over the line. He had a director that directed the actors. He would tell the director what he wanted, and the director would tell the actors, and we'd do the scene.

When we'd do the scene, we'd stand in the studio with a mike and script and watch the control booth. He'd stand in there. We'd work and we'd watch the control booth for cues and we'd act and cut. We'd watch the action in the control booth, and if Walt was pacing back and forth with his hands behind his back, shaking his head, we knew we were going to do it again. If he stood there with his hands folded across his chest or in his lap and nodding his head then it was a take. Then, the director would say, "Okay, that's a print," or "We're going to do it again." But Walt would never direct, never tell us what to do. He told the director, and the director told us.

One of my favorite scenes is when Pinocchio is at head of stairs and doesn't know what to do and starts, "I Got No Strings on Me," and trips and goes aaaaaahhhhh down the stairs and ends up with his nose in a knothole. I like that scene.

Snow White and the Seven Dwarfs *was a huge step for the Disney studio. That was their first full length color animation. Then, they started on* Bambi, *but they got* Pinocchio *in the middle of it. If you look at* Snow White *and then* Pinocchio, *boy! You'll see the quality that far surpassed anything in* Snow White. *You can tell it. Looks like real people doing real life stuff.*

They even went so far as to put an 8mm or a real small camera that was set up right in front of us and all it did was focus on our nose, mouth, and chin. Those are the three things that move when you're talking. To get it right, the animators had to see how the mouth would form the words.

Then, they got hung up on the "Hi diddle dee, an actor's life for me," where we skipped off down the road. The animators said they couldn't figure out the steps, the combination of movements, so they dressed us up in costume and built a set with a rolling rock road with a Swiss chalet behind and we acted that scene going down the road. "Hi diddle dee, an actor's life for me," and we skipped and went off down the road. They filmed that, and the animators looked at it and put it on the drawing board.

"I Got No Strings on Me." I didn't act that out because my head wouldn't turn and my body stand still.

The music for this picture was outstanding. Although neither "Hi Diddle Dee" nor "I Got No Strings on Me" received such recognition, "When You Wish Upon a Star" was the first aspect of an animated picture to win an Academy Award. The animation of the clocks in the workshop and the craftsmanship that made Pinocchio's movements to the song, "Little Wooden Head," are brilliant.

The one thing I didn't like was how they were trying to get Pinocchio to sound when he was talking under water. One of them was to lay me on a gurney and have me read the script and pour water in my mouth. They damned near drowned me. Someone finally had the idea of talking through a megaphone with a butterfly baffle on it. You talk into it and the butterfly would make the words go blublubblublublu. When they found that worked, they did it electronically.

Dick told me that his memories of the premiere of *Pinocchio* were basically a blur of activity. His date for the event was brought back into focus by an unearthed photograph. His date was Darla Hood, of the *Our Gang* shorts, and Dick reflected, at that time, he had something of a crush on her.

This friend of ours who works for the L.A. Times *was doing an interview when* Pinocchio *came out this last time, and searching through his archives, he came across a picture of Darla and me stepping out of our limousine at the premiere of* Pinocchio. *She was dressed up in a long formal evening gown with her hair up on top of her head.*

There were two other stars there, Hedy Lamarr and Constance Bennett, who had on the same evening gown [as Darla, as well as each other]. *Constance Bennett was usually a blonde, but she was a brunette that night. The publicity people kept them far apart—one on one side of the lobby and one on the other side. I walked into the lobby and saw Hedy Lamarr in her evening gown, and I said, "Wow!" I looked around and there she was on the other side. I found out later the two different women were dressed in the same gown.*

This last time Pinocchio *came out, they had two days of interviews. I was here at home, and they would call me and introduce themselves. I had the list of the people who were going to call. They came from all over the world.*

I didn't see Pinocchio *clear through until about five years ago. At the premiere, I was too busy to sit down and watch a movie. I didn't even see it put together after the premiere. I was going to see it when they had a party about the third or fourth time they renewed it. My granddaughter was five years old, and I had her sitting next to me in the studio theater. When Monstro the Whale jumped out of the water and was chasing us on the raft, she got scared silly, jumped up in the air, and buried her head into my coat, and I was trying to placate her and never saw the rest of the movie.*

This new Pinocchio [70th Anniversary edition] *is about the third time that they've completely redone* Pinocchio. *They had us over to the studio to preview it. They showed the original and then they showed the new. The new was brighter, sharper, better quality. The sound was greater, the music was clearer. It was like a brand spankin' new thing.*

I didn't see it clear through until this last time when they did all the new sound and revitalized the color. They've sharpened the color up. They've sharpened the sound up. It's absolutely pristine.

If they didn't keep restoring it, it would have died on the vine. Those colors fade away to nothing.

Dick enjoyed talking about work on *Pinocchio*. He was proud to be a part of such an innovative, ground-breaking labor of love that is recognized worldwide as a masterpiece. Being named a Disney Legend gratified him and he faithfully attended the events honoring and promoting the production whenever he was able. His experience working with his fellow cast members and the crew was one that he treasured. It was one of the highlights of his film career.

The Early 1940s

NONE OF THE NON-WESTERN FILMS that Dick appeared in before his radio years in the 1940s provided him with outstanding roles, though his performances were dead on at whatever character he portrayed. Several fall into the "as a boy" category, limiting his screen time.

In *Maryland,* Dick's role is brief. As eleven-year-old Lee Danfield, he comes in hiding his hand from his mother (Fay Bainter) because he injured it riding a horse. She had forbidden all horses on her property after her husband was killed from a horse fall. He immediately goes up to his room, and the next time we see young Lee Danfield, he has grown into John Payne.

Dick's role in *The Howards of Virginia* is that of young Matt Howard. He grows up to be Cary Grant. His ability to communicate sorrow probably played a part in being hired for this, as a major component was expressing grief when his father was killed in battle. He demonstrates his ability to cry on cue beautifully.

Although it is not marked with front titles, in the end titles, the cast from the early footage is separated as players in the "prologue."

The Howards of Virginia was memorable for Dick for a particular reason.

The Howards of Virginia was interesting. I worked with two different people who were supposed to be my father. They tested Forrest Tucker and Ralph Byrd, and I did the same scene with both of them. One of them would be cast as Cary Grant's [my] father.

Dick performs in a screen test with Forrest Tucker.

The Early 1940s

The Howards of Virginia **screen test with Ralph Byrd.**

I ended up keeping the costume from that. I don't know why. I had the jacket and the pants, but I didn't get to keep the coonskin cap. It was supposed to be in Virginia; we shot the whole thing up in Santa Cruz—just inland from the ocean. It was shot in the evening, and time off we'd go down to the fun zone and ride the roller coaster, shoot the targets at the shooting gallery. It was a fun job.

Adventure in Washington, also known as *Senate Pageboys*, used a lot of leftover footage from *Mister Smith Goes to Washington*, according to Dick. It was a story of a troubled boy for whom reform was planned by using the responsibility of being a Senate page.

Dick remembered making it, but was not impressed by it.

Adventure in Washington *was a spin-off of* Mister Smith Goes to Washington. *They used a lot of stock footage from* Mister Smith *with Herbert Marshall and Virginia Bruce* [as the stars]. *Gene Reynolds was in that and went on to be a big director. He did much of* M.A.S.H. *That's the same Gene Reynolds.*

No exciting memories of Adventure in Washington. *Stock shots from* Mister Smith Goes to Washington *and shots of fooling around in the dormitory with the other pageboys.* [Pause.] *That didn't sound right.*

In the classic crime movie, *This Gun for Hire*, with Veronica Lake, Robert Preston, and Alan Ladd, Ladd plays the killer, Raven, whose first kill was an aunt who abused him. In the widely available version of the film, Raven tells Ellen (Lake) the story of the aunt breaking his wrist with a hot iron and his fatal retaliation. But there are missing minutes. The sequence was actually filmed with Dick, playing Raven as a boy, and Hermine Sterler as the aunt in this dream/flashback sequence.

Dick remembered:

I played Alan Ladd in a dream sequence—five minutes of film. It was a dream with smoke on the floor—dry ice laid the fog on the floor—and explained how he got that deformed wrist. When Paramount sold it for syndication, they cut that five minutes out. The only way I can see it is to find somebody that got a copy that was distributed to the theaters before it was sold. That print will have eighty-six rather than eighty-one minutes.

They used smoke pots like they use for getting bees to go to sleep when they rob their hives in the filming of my scene in This Gun for Hire. *They'd run it over dry ice and it forms a cloud on the ground and just stays there for a long time and we had to do all the action moving around in that fog stuff. It explained how he got the big lump on his wrist.*

I've seen long versions of that on the credits and I'm on the credits even though I'm not in that version.

At the time of his death, neither Dick nor I had been able to find a copy of the longer, full-length version of *This Gun for Hire* for purchase or rental.

The Vanishing Virginian is the tale of the ups and downs of a family in the early years of the twentieth century. The patriarch, Robert Yancey (Frank Morgan), is a lawyer. His wife, Rosa (Spring Byington), flits around, a delightful ditz, who calls her husband, "Mr. Yancey." Dick plays Robert Yancey, Jr., the older son of the family. It's a pleasant outing, but the only

The Early 1940s

outstanding marks for Dick are playing the banjo as the family sings and the brouhaha about his bloody nose.

Robert, Jr. (Dick Jones), Joel (Scotty Beckett), Robert, Sr., (Frank Morgan), Caroline (Juanita Quigley), and Rosa (Spring Byington) Yancey gather around the breakfast table in *The Vanishing Virginian*.

Several of the actors in the movie had shared or would share screen credits with Dick, such as Juanita Quigley, who played his younger sister in *The Vanishing Virginian* and the girl member of the gang in *Devil's Party*.

I don't remember a lot about The *Vanishing Virginian. There were a lot of people there, and I remember the actor Frank Morgan real well. He was pleasant to work with. I don't have a lot of memories from it. There were too many kids and we were all tied up with the school teacher. We'd come on the set, do our job. They'd tell us, "Do this, do that." We'd do it and then go back to school. Wasn't Kathryn Grayson in that?*

Spring Byington. What a lovely lady she was! She was so cute. A little bitty thing. She was the same off-stage as she was on-stage—real sweet and peppy. Perky. I liked her very much.

Dick once commented to me, "I've got a still from *Maryland* with all of them gathered around me. I have a bloody nose and they're all trying to console me for getting bopped in the nose." We did not locate this still, and the scene is actually from *The Vanishing Virginian*. There is no bloody nose in *Maryland*.

Mountain Rhythm was a wartime film starring the Weaver Brothers and Elviry. The Weavers move to California to help the war effort, but locate next to a snobby boys' prep school with an institution-wide arrogance toward those who work with their hands. The snobbishness has an underlying, treasonous motive which must be dealt with before all can end well. Dick played one of the schoolboys.

Mountain Rhythm *was just a two- or three-day job for the whole picture. We had a lot of fun in the cantaloupe field busting up cantaloupes, shooting them like playing polo, batting the ball around. We had a bunch of saddle falls on that thing because there were wickets out there around the cantaloupes and you'd hit them with the mallet and it would jerk us off the horse. I think that's one I did for Republic. That's one* [film] *I don't have.*

The Adventures of Mark Twain is a dramatization of the life of Samuel Clemens, aka Mark Twain, from his childhood days on the Mississippi River to his death. Starting as a flashback narrated by Twain (Fredric March) after his death and ending with him ascending into the afterlife at "The End," it hits the highlights of his adventurous life. If it stretches the truth, well, Twain himself admonished that the truth could be overused.

Starting with the baby, four actors play Samuel Clemens/Mark Twain in the film: Fredric March for most of it, the baby, Jackie Brown at age twelve, and Dick Jones at age fifteen.

Dick plays Sam at a rebellious point, when he leaves home for the river. We see him working in the print shop, a job the twelve-year-old Sam promised he would give a try. It is not going well. He can't seem to learn the ropes and longs to be anywhere else.

Dick does an outstanding job of expressing discontent with facial expressions and body language, as well as his lines. With no sense of propriety, he pulls a prank by printing a farcical story in the paper and flees the office when the subject of the article enters raging.

Leaving a note on his mother's pillow, he heads for the river with the goal of being a riverboat pilot. Our last view of Dick as Sam is with Captain Bixby (Robert Barrat) berating him for his failure to pick up skills needed to safely steer the boat. Though the captain yells for Sam to go, he calls him back saying that he said he would train him, and he will. As Dick grasps the wheel, he fades and then March takes over the role.

I remember getting to drive the steamboat and getting cussed out by the captain, Robert Barrat. When I was at the wheel, he was cussing me out because I was getting too close to the sandbars. It was done on a set with a processed scene behind. I had to cry. They were going to blow onion juice in my eyes to make me cry, and I said, "No, I can do it. I'm a good actor." I thought about my favorite book that every time I think about it, I cry. So, I stood there with my hands on the spokes of the wheel, looking down the river and tears coming out of my eyes, and fade out. And the next thing you see, I'm not there, and it's Fredric March.

Heaven Can Wait starred Don Ameche as Henry Van Cleve, who upon dying presents himself to the Devil (Laird Cregar) because he knows he is Hell-bound. The Devil isn't prepared for his appearance, so Henry tells him his life story, beginning with his baby carriage days.

By his teen years (Dickie Moore plays fifteen-year-old Henry), he is well on his way to being a spoiled rich roué. On the morning of his fifteenth birthday, Henry is too hung over from drinking champagne with the French maid the night before to get out of bed. The family thinks he's sick, but can't understand a word he says in his "delirium" because he's speaking French.

Dick is terrific as Henry's teenage Cousin Albert, who sets the record straight by priggishly translating the French and blowing the whistle on his cousin. His screen time is brief—at Albert's next appearance, he has become Allyn Joslyn—but he has a nice scene with Charles Coburn (Grandpa Van Cleve). Dick nails the attitude perfectly.

They had me dressed up in a Lord Fauntleroy costume with the knicker pants and a big collar, and I was getting chewed out because I let Dickie Moore, who was supposed to be my brother, get drunk. He was messing around with Signe Hasso—I think she was supposed to be the maid. My line was something about he dropped a quarter in her décolletage and complained because no candy bar came out. I was Allyn Joslyn as a kid. Don Ameche was the star of that one. Dickie Moore played Don Ameche as a kid. Other than the Our Gang *comedies, that's the only time Dickie Moore and I worked together.*

Actually, it was not Dick's job to keep his cousin from getting drunk, he just happened to know that Henry and the French maid went out on the town and drank champagne. Albert (Dickie) can't wait to rat out his cousin and tell that he dropped a nickel down the décolletage of a prominent society matron. Albert is a prude, and his grandfather's response to the little killjoy brings a laugh.

And he and Dickie Moore worked together several times.

On the Air

MANY FANS THINK OF DICK AS STRICTLY a big screen and television performer, but also he had radio experience.

In addition to his previously mentioned preschooler work on the *Cowboy Ramblers Radio Show* before he moved from Texas, he worked a couple of shows that did stick in his memory.

From the 1930s to the 1950s, a popular radio program for many listeners was the *Lux Radio Theatre*. The goal of this anthology series was to bring noted stories to the ear of the public. Early episodes adapted plays, but soon motion pictures became the source for live broadcasts that featured the stars recreating their roles on the screen.

In *Stella Dallas* (the movie), Dick had portrayed Lee Morrison, a son of

Helen (Barbara O'Neil), whom Stephen Dallas (John Boles) marries after he and Stella (Barbara Stanwyck) break up.

In late 1937, when *Stella Dallas* was adapted for the *Lux Radio Theatre*, Dick was one of the players who brought his on-screen role to the living rooms of America. This was his first national radio experience.

Dick would return to radio for a longer run, when he played one of the most beloved characters of the Golden Age of Radio, Henry Aldrich.

One of the top radio comedies in the 1940s was *The Aldrich Family*, often remembered by fans as Henry Aldrich. The character originated in a Broadway play by Clifford Goldsmith, *What a Life*.

Stories focused on the teenage son of the Aldrich family, Henry. The introduction, with his mother calling, "Hen-reeeeeee. Hen-ry Al-drich," and his reply, "Coming, Mother," became one of the most recognizable openings in radio history.

The first radio sketches were created for Rudy Vallee's radio show by the playwright, Goldsmith. The sketches moved to *The Kate Smith Hour* before the characters gained their own radio time slot as *The Aldrich Family*. The series had a long run, from the early sketches in 1938 to the final program in 1953.

The Aldrich Family ranked high in the ratings. The hit show was competitive for top place for a number of years of its run. Goldsmith was said to be the highest-paid writer in radio at the time. The public loved Henry's antics and teenage problems, tuning in faithfully to hear the next episode.

Dick was one of several actors who portrayed Henry, who was first brought to life by Ezra Stone, both on Broadway and on radio. Dick's shows were during the World War II years, and the Henrys kept leaving for the armed services.

Dick remembered his years on the show:

There's a lot I remember about the radio years. It's an altogether different story. My whole life was different then. That's [radio] *a whole different ball of wax as far as movies are concerned.*

I would not live on Manhattan Island, number one, so I went to a private school in upstate New York. I would come down to Manhattan to do the radio show one day a week.

I'd come in in the evening, and we'd sit down and read the next week's story, and the next day, we'd start before breakfast and go all day long, and we'd do two shows in the evening—one for back East and one for the West Coast two or three hours later. Then, I'd run like hell to get out of Rockefeller Center, way up on the fiftieth floor—or something like that—and hope the elevator would work. Then, I'd catch a cab that was waiting for me. (They'd have a cab sitting there waiting.) I'd catch the last train out of Grand Central Station to go back to Tarrytown, and there'd be a cab sitting there waiting to take me back up to school.

The next day, Thursday or Friday, the show was on Wednesday or Thursday [Thursday, at that point.], I'd still have a day or two of school to go. They didn't give me any slack at all as far as schoolwork was concerned.

Henry Aldrich was such a short stint in my life that I was busier than a cat on a tin roof between shows and I only did the show one day and a couple of hours the night before. It was a tough job.

We always read it. You don't do a radio show without reading your script because you can't have dead air. Playing in front of an audience, we didn't have those big guffaw, hurrah, ha-ha-ha things that go on and on and on so it didn't slow the show down.

It was funny but mild funny.

It was live radio. We did it in front of a live audience.

Some of the things working in front of live audiences were distracting, like I'd have to be dressed up in slacks and a jacket with a tie. I remember jumping up onto the stage. They'd do the intro. She'd say, "Hen-reeeee! Hen-ry Al-drich!" and I'd say, "Coming, Mother" and I'd run out and jump onto the stage and [one night] *the fly on my slacks broke—the zipper just went—and there I was trying to keep my back to the audience and continue with the show because there wasn't time to slow down and get it fixed.*

Another time, I'm working with Jackie Kelk. He had an easel and I had an easel. We were face-to-face, and the mike was in the middle, and my pages were all on cardboard so there wouldn't be the rustling of the pages in the microphone and

I slipped it over to the next one and it was out of place—or wasn't there—and I just froze.

Jackie saw that horrified look in my face and he came around and put his script up in front of me and we finished that one scene and, I mean, I thought there was about an hour between when I found out I didn't have the page and the time Kelk put it in front of me, but when we listen to it, you wouldn't think there was a drop in the lines.

Jackie Kelk and Dick Jones appear as Homer and Henry Aldrich for the radio show, *The Aldrich Family*.

It was strictly a family show—no guests. It was Henry's father, mother, sister, and best friend, Homer, and then maybe a couple of people would come in and play parts like a schoolteacher or a coach or something like that. Nobody got any credit for the thing except Henry Aldrich and Jackie Kelk, who played Homer.

When Uncle Sam caught me, Jackie Kelk stepped in and played Henry Aldrich for the rest of the season. There were four Henry Aldriches. [Actually more than that: Ezra Stone, Norman Tokar, Dick Jones, Kelk, Raymond Ives, Stone again, and Bobby Ellis.] *Norman Tokar was the second one. When Norman got drafted, they got me up there. They tested and they got me and Richard Crenna. I got the part, and they said, "We don't want you to imitate Henry Aldrich, we want you to change the whole thing and you're going to be yourself.*

Clifford Goldsmith, the author, took me up to his place at Martha's Vineyard up in Massachusetts, near the ocean. He had a house up there. He kept me up there for a month or so, and day in and day out, he drilled me on who Henry Aldrich was and the inflections of a teenager's voice. "A teenager," he would say, "will always end on an up-note whereas an adult goes down at the end of a sentence." It was stuff like that that he drilled me on. I didn't try to imitate the original Henry Aldrich. It was me.

When we'd get together the night before the show to read the script for the story for the week following, I'd recognize that Clifford Goldsmith (he had a memory like an elephant) had developed things I had told him about high school in Henry Aldrich shows a couple of times. . . . I remembered telling him about my high school stuff.

I remembered my escapades that I told him that he dressed up and made into a Henry Aldrich show. I recognized what had happened to me, and I said, "Hey, you're using my stuff!" and he said, "Well, certainly. Why did you think I did it? [He talked to Dick extensively about his high school.]

There was one in particular, the time that I was going to a track meet. I was a pole vaulter and I had to take my pole with me. I had this 16-foot pole, and there was no baggage car on the train, so I had to get it into the passenger car. It didn't want to bend around the corner.

You try to get a 16-foot bamboo pole that's about 3 inches in diameter into a railroad car—a passenger car. They opened up a couple of windows and I was able to get it in there. He [Goldsmith] *made something hilariously funny out of it.*

I remember that one real well. It turned out to be a funny, funny show.

The most fun about it was we could keep checking with the Crossley judging the popularity of the shows. It was either Jack Benny or Fibber McGee and Molly *that we were trying to top. We got ahead of Jack Benny one time for a month or two, but we never could get ahead of* Fibber McGee and Molly.

Henry Aldrich got a few ratings I was pretty proud of. For a while, it was number two nighttime show.

I did radio for two and half years. That was before I got tangled up with Autry. I did that until Uncle Sam caught me and shipped me overseas to Alaska. I did go overseas. At that time, it was a possession of the United States not part of the United States.

A number of the radio episodes with the voice of Dick Jones, including his reprise of the *Stella Dallas* role, were available for purchase and through streaming on the Internet at the time of the original publication date of this book.

Returning to Film

AFTER HIS SERVICE IN WORLD WAR II, DICK returned to California to work again in film. It was an uphill job. Leaving film for the East Coast and radio had put him in a bad light with some film industry powers. He never worked at 20th Century Fox again.

In 1948, Gene Autry tapped him for a role in *The Strawberry Roan*. Dick said, "*The Strawberry Roan* is the show that got me back into show business." It was far from his favorite of the films he did, but he recognized its position in his career.

I just don't like that movie. However, it was the first color that Gene did at Columbia, and I worked in that one, and I ended up, after five or six years, I did his last movie at Columbia, Last of the Pony Riders. *But Gene got me back in the business.*

Dick ended up contracted to Autry—a rare happening in Dick's long career in film—and appeared in several of Autry's last films, as well as worked on television for his Flying A Productions.

For the most part, the films in which Dick appeared as an adult may be classified as Western or war. He had few comments to make about them, generally something about the people on the set.

On *The Strawberry Roan*:

I remember working with Jack Holt. I worked with him several times. He was a fine actor and a real good mechanic. He was fun to work with because he knew what he was doing. I didn't have to feed him his lines.

I think that was Pat Buttram's first movie with Gene. He was funny as all get-out when he was in a good mood. Sometimes, he wouldn't even say hello to you. But he was fun to work with when he was in a good mood.

Once, I was with him on a question and answer panel up at Lone Pine. We were in the school auditorium, which was right on a highway. Just Pat and I were up on the stage talking about Gene, and the Highway Patrol went screaming by chasing somebody. Pat leaned over and whispered in my ear, but it came over the microphone, "Well, there goes Gene on his way to the bank."

On *Sons of New Mexico*:

Russell Ward was the one I remember the most. He was the one that did all the singing on the Lucky Strike Theatre. *He was a headline crooner. This was one of his first pictures, and he had to do a fight scene with me. So, that was fun, choreographing that one so he didn't get hurt.*

I admired the way Frankie Darro could tumble. Damn! He could jump up straight from a standstill and do a back flip. He could do back handsprings. I couldn't do it without spraining an ankle— or a wrist, which is worse than spraining an ankle.

On *Redwood Forest Trail*:

I worked with Alfalfa [Carl Switzer from the *Our Gang* shorts] *in a Rex Allen show. He was Rex Allen's sidekick for a while. I remember we played a trick on Jeff Donnell. We were shooting up at a campgrounds in San Bernardino Mountains. We had a gag where Rex Allen gets knocked off his horse when they string a rope across the trail and they used a dummy to get knocked off. The dummy was just sitting on the prop truck dressed up like Rex.*

Jeff Donnell went to the privy. Alfie and I get the dummy and go up there and yell, "Come out or I'm coming in."

She yells, "Don't you dare come in here," and we opened up the door and threw Rex Allen in there.

You should have heard her scream. Boy! She let out a scream that would have scared everybody off the mountain. She comes running out, "I'll kill you, you sons of a bitches." She chased us all over that campground.

On *Last of the Pony Riders*:

Of all the films I did for Autry, I liked Last of the Pony Riders *best. There was some good action in it. I thought the story was good, and I enjoyed working with my good friend, Buzz Henry.*

On *The Wild Dakotas*:

That was with Bill Williams. Bill Williams was a great guy.

On *Shadow of a Boomerang*:

I got two trips to Australia on that one. For some reason, we got down there and had to turn right around and come back. Then, about a month or six weeks later, off we go again. I go down and am there maybe three months. Seemed more like six months. We worked all over the Outback—twenty-five to fifty miles out into nothing.

It was a real good evangelistic-type picture. I had a good part in it.

Dick had a longer tale of *Sands of Iwo Jima*.

I made more money on Sands of Iwo Jima *than anything I ever did. I was cast for a part in it. I got a contract out of it; got wardrobe; got script. Then, two or three days before going on location, the agent called up and said, "You've been cut out of that, but you got paid." So, they had to pay me off for the contract—minimum on that—paid me off for wardrobe, paid me off for the script. So, I got two or three weeks of pay right there for nothing.*

Then, about two or three weeks into the shooting of the thing down at Camp

Pendleton down at San Diego, Allan Dwan says, "I want that kid back for that part." (Backtrack—Herbert Yates says, "We're gonna hafta cut the budget on this thing. We're going to rip out everything that isn't necessary for the picture." That's when I got eliminated.)

Dwan says, "I want this part back in and I want that kid back in," so, I got a call.

"Yeah, I'm available."

"We'll hire you on a daily. You go down to San Diego on a daily because it's just an hour's work."

I was down there two weeks, and every day was an overtime day. On Saturday and Sunday, it went into golden time, and I was just sitting around there watching the scenery go by and the shooting and stuff like that. I was just a spectator until my time came to do it and I came crashing into the wave, dove in alongside Wayne, went berserk and jumped up and ran out and they rat-a-tat-tat, shot me.

I made more money on that picture than any other picture I ever did. I spent two weeks down at Pendleton for fifteen minutes.

Dick did not find film work as lucrative as he desired. He told me that with a wife and children, he wanted something more dependable, so he turned to the financial/real estate industry. Nevertheless, he never officially retired from acting and kept his SAG card the rest of his life.

On the Rock

When Dick was asked to name his favorite of the films he appeared in or one that was memorable for him, *Rocky Mountain* is first on the list.

This Civil War film begins with tourists stopping to read an historical marker. Fade to the tale with introductory narration by Captain Lafe Barstow (Errol Flynn).

A dark and heavy score by Max Steiner signals the coming drama and tragedy.

Eight men led by Barstow have been sent to California on a mission to save the Confederacy. They meet with a man, Cole Smith (Howard Petrie), who is supposed to bring them to people in California sympathetic to the Southern cause. But before negotiations can be completed, they are sidetracked by an Indian attack on a stagecoach. This movie goes to show what happens when you don't stay on task.

In a great action scene (Yakima Canutt coordinated the stunt work) the men run off the Indians and rescue a woman passenger, Johanna Carter (Patrice Wymore), the fiancée of a Yankee Lieutenant Rickey (Scott Forbes). He will come searching for his woman.

When Rickey and the men and the scouts with him locate the Rebels, Johanna begs Barstow not to kill her fiancé, so the gallant captain tries to take them hostage. The Yankees and their Indian scouts become captives.

The California emissary leaves to bring back his men. In the night, one of the Indian scouts escapes, and now everything depends on the Californians arriving before the Indians attack. The lieutenant wants to go for help from a Union garrison but after his avowal to escape if possible, Barstow refuses. Rickey gets away in the night.

Then, a loose horse wanders toward camp. When they pick it up, it is the one Cole Smith was riding. As the Indians move closer to attack, the Confederates opt to ride out and lead the Indians away from the woman, the stage driver (Chubby Johnson), and the remaining Yankee captive. It works, but they ride into a rock wall and decide to charge the Indians and make an open battle of it rather wait for the attack.

When they ride out, Buck/Jim (Dick Jones) leaves his dog, Spot, with Johanna before the group leads the Indians away. However, Spot jumps from her arms and follows the men into battle.

The Cavalry arrives in time to save the woman, but not in time to save the group of Confederate men. The Southerners go hand-to-hand with the Indians, but overwhelmingly outnumbered, all die. The Cavalry gets there in time to show respect for the dead.

There's a nice scene for Dick, when he takes Johanna a plate of black-eyed peas and tells her the story about giving some to Robert E. Lee at Gettysburg.

He has some good dialog with Flynn, too. For a sixteen-year-old who volunteered for the Southern army at age fourteen, Buck has plenty of personal history to tell, including why he wants to be called Jim instead of his given name, Buck.

He also has an impressive gag being knocked from his horse and killed with an arrow.

For this rough, heavy action film, several real horsemen held lead roles. Dick (Buck/Jim Wheat) had been riding since he could walk. Buzz Henry (Kip Waterson) also rode from his first years. Horsebacker Guinn "Big Boy" Williams, billed here as Guinn, (Pap Dennison) played polo. Slim Pickens (Plank) came from rodeo.

Dick loved to talk about making *Rocky Mountain*.

They put me under contract for Rocky Mountain *about two or three weeks before the show actually started because Buzz and I had to test all the people who were being contemplated for riding and we showed them what was expected of them. Buzz Henry and I sure raised hell up in Gallop, New Mexico, on* Rocky Mountain.

When they shot me in Rocky Mountain *with an arrow, they were going to have me do it down a wire. Shoot the arrow down a wire into the chest plate.*

I said, "Not on your life. Because you're going to have to wrap that around me about three times, and when I come off the horse and roll into the camera, that wire could get kinked, and when it gets a kink in it, that arrow coming down is going to break the wire and that arrow's going to go anywhere other than to the chest plate."

They said, "The only other way is to get an archer to shoot a real arrow."

I said, "Get Howard Hill."

The next thing I know, they fly in Howard Hill.

I said, "Are you in good shape?"

He said, "Yeah."

I said, "Do me the ring trick."

So, he throws a ring out and Bang! shoots the arrow through it. And he did that three out of three times, and I said, "Okay, let's shoot it."

So, I came off the horse, came up and drew my gun, and Bam! He got me right in the chest plate.

People said, "That's scary."

I said, "I wasn't worried."

He was a phenom.

I see that thing [gag from *Rocky Mountain*] in half a dozen shows—in *Mavericks* a couple of times. I see it several times in *Cheyenne*. Where we charge into the Indians and one of them comes running up to me—he's got a tomahawk, I think—and is going to hack me down and I just drop over the side and he swings at nothing and I come up and knock him off his horse, shooting him, then I come back up on the horse and go on.

We had to do that a half a dozen times because the damn horse was outrunning the camera car. He was a real fast horse—quarter horse. His name was Copper. He would let me trick ride all over him. He was real sturdy. I had to have a horse that was strong because when I fell off on the side like that and come up under him if the horse stumbled and goes down where does he land? On me. And I didn't want that to happen. So, I had to be very careful choosing my horse.

[Yakima Canutt] . . . *was a master at rigging stuff.*

In *Rocky Mountain* the director said, "I want the wagon dumped right there. X marks the spot."

Yak says, "Fine. Move your camera."

The cameraman says, "No, that's my spot. I'm going to photograph that coming right into me."

Yak says, "That's right. It gonna be right into you."

They came to an impasse and the director says, "Stop the haggling and let's go."

Yak says, "Don't say I didn't warn you." So he rolled over three times—over, over, BANG! Right on top of that $35,000 camera.

Yak says, "I warned you. X marks the spot. X marks the spot is where it's gonna be."

I went down to the pound with the director and found the dog for *Rocky Mountain*.

The director took me down to the pound and said, "We got to find a dog for you for this show that will be your dog and is photogenic."

We didn't have to look too far. We found this dog that was half Spitz, half Samoyed, which turned out to be Spot, and he liked me, and the director thought he was photogenic, and he said, "This is your dog. You have to feed him. You have to take care of him. Don't let anybody else touch him. Don't let anybody else feed him. Don't let them play with him. He's your dog."

So, I kept him all that time. We had to get a special dispensation at the Rancho Hotel in Gallup so I could keep the dog in my room.

They said, "We don't allow animals in the rooms."

The director said, "How much does it cost to renovate that room if we put the dog in?"

I don't know what they paid, but he stayed in my room all the time.

The cutest part about the whole thing was this theme song the dog had. Every time he'd run across the screen, they'd play this funny little music.

Spot, the show stealer.

At the end when the U.S. Cavalry arrives too late to save the hero, we all lay down in our spots where we were supposed to be dead, and I had the dog under my arm, and when they decided to get ready to go, the handler came in and took the *dog away from me. Then, I switched spots with somebody else on the other side of the battlefield.*

So, when they came over the hill to find everybody dead, the dog came over and he couldn't find me. He went from one guy to the other guy trying to find me, and when he found me, he bowed his head like he was crying. He was very good. He was very photogenic. Spot stole the show.

When they made the Cheyenne [television episode], *they used all of those back shots, horse shots, and Indian fight shots from* Rocky Mountain, *and the dog was very prominent. So, they hired my dog. But I didn't have the right card, I couldn't take him to the studio. I couldn't handle him. I didn't belong to the teamsters union, so they hired a teamster and sent him over in a chauffeur-driven limousine. He would come up to the door and pick up the dog and take him on a leash out to the car, and at 6 o'clock at night, he'd bring him back, and all the neighbors would look out the window. What's going on? How come the dog is going to work in a limousine and Dick's still at home?*

Spot was a good dog—good around the kids.

I took him on the promotional tour when we premiered that thing in Colorado Springs. Had to get special permission to take him on the train—keep him in the stateroom—and special permission for him to stay in the hotel room in Colorado Springs. He was a more of a celebrity than the celebrities were.

All my kids remember Spot.

Dick made a few random comments about his memories from the film.

We did not do a lot of night shots on Rocky Mountain. *They used a night lens. They wanted the clouds to show. We did some of it at night. It was nicer to work at night because it wasn't as hot.*

That movie almost goes down in history a couple of times. It's one of the few pictures that was shot entirely exterior, no interior shots, and it was the first time in the history of the United States motion picture industry that the U.S. Cavalry arrived too late to save the hero.

They used lots of real Indians in the picture. In the fight scenes, most of the "Indians" were Hollywood stuntmen.

Dick's wife, Betty, was a big Errol Flynn fan. When Flynn learned this, he and Dick set up a prank to play on her at the *Rocky Mountain* wrap-up party at Flynn's house.

They set up a signal for Dick to make when he and Betty got to the party. When Dick and Betty arrived, Dick signaled and Flynn came from the house to greet them.

He took Betty's hand in his, kissed it gallantly, and spoke flowery words indicating he had been waiting all evening just to see her.

Betty told me, "I swooned."

The autographed still Errol Flynn gave Betty and Dick.

It is no wonder Dick enjoyed making this film so much. He was working with men he liked, who were as action-oriented as he was. The camaraderie was good. Spot, the dog who was his constant companion in the show, became the family dog at the Jones house during the years when his children were growing up. It was an outdoor movie, all exteriors, and films shot largely off the sound stage were Dick's favorite to shoot. It was almost as if *Rocky Mountain* was designed to please Dick Jones.

Cool, Man, Cool

MADE IN 1958, *The Cool and the Crazy* is typical of the drug-scare films of the era. Think *High School Confidential, The Blackboard Jungle,* and the earlier *Reefer Madness.*

Bennie (Scott Marlowe) is the new kid, straight from reform school, who comes in on his first day disrupting class with wisecracks and defiant behavior.

The boys in the school are no angels, quickly jumping in with smart remarks of their own. Stu (Dick Jones) is one of the leaders. He is mean in this picture. (His wife, Betty, didn't like to watch him in those kinds of roles, and neither do I.)

Jackie (Dick Bakalyan) is the clown, constantly changing best buds in order to be liked. Amy, the girlfriend Jackie picks up at a dance (Gigi Perreau), tells him that he's really not bad, the other boys are a bad influence on him. She's kidding herself.

After class, the other boys hassle Bennie, verbally and physically. He takes it as a sign that they are ready to try and get hooked on drugs, so he makes a beeline for his drug source, Eddie (Marvyn J. Rosen, in his only recorded screen appearance).

Eddie is not convinced but agrees to supply "the smoke." Bennie's goal is to soon hook them on "the needle."

Jackie (Dick Bakalyan) and Stu (Dick Jones) hang out at Pat's Pig.

That evening, Bennie shows up at Pat's Pig, the teenage hangout. The boys start on him again, but he throws out some intriguing remarks and drives away. They pile into the car and follow. Bennie goes to the police station.

In a scene that borders on the absurd, he makes a scene in front of the police. Stu and Jackie are watching from outside with dropping jaws. Figuring Ben will be arrested, they get out of there, but the police—unbelievably—kick him out and tell him to go home.

Bennie catches up with the group and gives them beer. Stu remains aloof and does not join in. Ben tells him that he's ready from something better and gives him a marijuana cigarette. That Stu takes.

Jackie (Dick Bakalyan) and Stu (Dick Jones) disagree.

Dick's performance as Stu on drugs is quite a production. He bangs his head on the table, staggers around the dance hall—the next stop of the night—and finally goes outside to bring back a bus stop sign for a dance partner. He does an excellent job of playing stoned, though the actions would be more appropriate for a junkie on hard drugs.

The next morning, all the boys are hung over. Instead of wanting a break, they all want more of the drug. One, Charlie Tyler, whom they all call "Cookie" (Robert Hadden, also in his only credited screen appearance), needs it so bad that he's planning to rob a gas station to get money for it. Once Bennie hooked them with one free reefer, he then wants money to supply it.

Bennie goes to Eddie to get more dope, but Eddie won't give it to him. Bennie himself is hooked, and in desperation for the drug, kills Eddie and takes the stash.

Meanwhile, Cookie has been killed trying to hold up the gas station. Despite the misfortune Bennie has brought, Jackie agrees to meet him when he calls. Stu, Amy, and one of the other boys go with him.

Bennie is stoned. When he drives toward them going to the meeting place, he drives straight at their car. They swerve to the side in time to miss his car, which goes off the road, crashes, and burns.

By this time, the police have finally gotten involved. While they all stand there watching the car burn, the lieutenant preaches to the survivors on the dangers of drugs.

As the film ends, Jackie says things will be okay now that Bennie is dead.

Dick had some standout memories of this film, even though he wasn't especially fond of it.

Of all the Westerns William Witney did, I never worked with him in a Western. So, I end up getting a part with him in a teenage, juvenile jive, marijuana bustin' party. I was really hooked on the stuff and he had me try to climb through the footwork on a desk. That was quite a job.

I just couldn't believe after all the times I wanted to work with him because he was considered a real good director of action Westerns I had to work with him in that thing.

Dick really wanted to do the car crash gag.

I did my best trying to sell Bill Witney on the fact that I could save him a lot of money if he'd let me roll the car.

He said, "No. I've got a stunt driver that's a professional at that."

I said, "I know how to do it." But he wouldn't let me do it.

He liked to tell the "almost jailed" story.

I almost got thrown in jail working on that show. We were working at night. We were in a car and they showed us a couple of blocks down and said to wait there until they gave us the cue to come screaming around the corner and down and brake and slide the car into the camera.

So, we're sitting down at the end of the street, two or three blocks away from where the shooting was. We're sitting in the car, lights out, motor running, and these cops pull up alongside of us. They want identification and to know what we're doing there, how come we're sitting there with the lights out and the motor running. And we had no explanation other than we're working in that picture down there.

"Yeah, sure you are."

"We're going to be doing this scene."

"Yeah, sure you are. From the jailhouse you're gonna do that scene."

They had us out of our car, just ready to hook us up and put us in their car, and the assistant director came down there and said, "I've got a change of plans."

And the cops said, "You sure do. You're not using these guys."

I almost got nailed on that one, but the assistant director had enough ID on him to straighten it out.

We didn't have anything. You don't carry you're ID around with you when you're working in a picture. I guess we should have had driver's licenses, but we didn't. It was close.

The Cool and the Crazy is a difficult film to find and not very likeable, but it provides its own type of entertainment—dated, cheesy, and kind of fun even with the violent and unbelievable aspects of the story—or maybe because of them.

Old Gunslingers

Dick's last credited film was *Requiem for a Gunfighter*. Made in 1965, the film was something of a last stand for a number of actors from the heyday of cowboy movies. Even the director, Spencer Gordon Bennet, hailed from the day of B-Westerns and cliffhanger serials. Among the actors were seasoned Western regulars Tim McCoy, Johnny Mack Brown, Bob Steele, Lane Chandler, Dale Van Sickle, Frank Lackteen, Raymond Hatton, Rand Brooks, Tom Steele, Zon Murray, Edmund Cobb, and Herman Hack.

Rod Cameron stars as Dave McCloud, a hired gun. He believes in gun law because "the law" hasn't reached "this area" yet. He's hired to execute the bad men, or so he sees it.

When he rides into town to kill, he does it with flare, riding into the saloon on his horse and dropping money by the body to pay for the burial. Cliff Fletcher (Dick Jones) vows to follow him to the next town and kill him in a gunfight. The young gunman wants to make his reputation by taking on McCloud in River Falls.

McCloud doesn't go where Cliff thinks he will. He's sidetracked by Judge Irving Short (Tim McCoy), who travels part of the road with him. There are some nice scenes with Rod Cameron and Tim McCoy. The Judge is on his way to Stopover Flats, Arizona, to preside over a murder trial. Red Zimmer (Stephen McNally) controls the town and his murderous crew takes anything he wants with guns and brutality. Zimmer sends Max Smith (Bob Steele) to kill the judge, which he does just after McCloud and Short part ways.

McCloud hears the shots, chases Max, and fatally wounds him, then goes back to bury the judge and take his papers. He changes his plans in order to go in and bring the judge's killer to justice.

When Zimmer mistakes McCloud for the judge and McCloud sees the evil in the town, he goes along with Zimmer's misapprehension in hopes of cleaning up the town for the decent people.

He considers that he might do for this town what he says he does in his job, only with the law rather than his gun.

Believing him to be Judge Short, Zimmer is after him from the start. His henchman Ivy Bliss (Mike Mazurki) wants to shoot the judge outright but Zimmer insists they must play it smart.

With the help of a young couple, Larry and Bonnie Young (Chet Douglas and Olive Sturgess), McCloud studies the judge's law book and holds a trial.

Zimmer controls the testimony, speaking for the defendant and blaming the death on Max, who is no longer alive to defend himself. Zimmer claims that he was in the saloon the whole time, but young Billy Parker (Chris Hughes) was in the back room and saw the whole thing.

When the trial recesses, McCloud and the Youngs learn that Billy was there. As Billy begins to testify, Zimmer loses his control and is disrupting the trial with his hysterical rants when Fletcher walks into the saloon/courtroom.

He sees McCloud over the batwing doors and breaks up the proceedings just as the truth is coming out.

Dick remembered this entry with a red face.

I felt so silly after doing that one scene when I come into the bar and I'm shouting "I'm the greatest," making a big hurrah, and I was spinning double guns up in the air and over my ear, in my face so the camera would pick it up, and around this guy that was standing there looking at me, and he said, "That's pretty good kid," and I'm right in the face of Johnny Mack Brown. Hell, he's one the best gun-spinners that ever was. I looked at who that was and just about fell through the floor. I was so embarrassed. I'm making a fool of myself showing off to him.

Even though the role called for it, I could have toned it down some—less braggadocio.

Cliff Fletcher (Dick Jones) flashes his guns in the face of the bailiff, Enkoff (Johnny Mack Brown), when he enters the saloon.

Brown plays Enkoff, the storekeeper who is serving as the bailiff. When Fletcher bursts into the trial, he immediately tries to subdue him, but

Fletcher's assertion that the judge is really Dave McCloud, the gunfighter, turns the whole room into chaos.

Zimmer tries to use the truth about the man presiding to his advantage but the crowd rises up against the villains who have abused them and take them off—to jail or to a lynching is not totally clear.

In the midst of the uproar, Fletcher challenges McCloud to a gunfight and the two of them recess to the street, followed by the crowd.

When they draw, McCloud shoots both guns from Fletcher's hands then shoots off his gun belt. When Fletcher declines to take the fight further, McCloud mounts his horse and leaves the town, hopefully to become a better place than he found it.

Dick remembered:

At the end of it, I turn cowardly, and Rod Cameron shoots the guns off my hips, and I turn and run. That took a lot of acting on my part.

Sometimes, all [the old cowboy stars] *were there together; sometimes one at a time. I was impressed with Col. Tim McCoy. He was at that time still straight as an arrow—still had his military bearing and carriage. Johnny Mack Brown and the others. It was fun.*

Jones & Jones

TWO OF DICK'S LAST THREE FILMS involved collaboration between L. Q. Jones and Alvy Moore. Simplified, Jones directed and Moore was one of the producers.

The first was a potboiler, *The Devil's Bedroom*, starring John Lupton, known to television viewers as Tom Jeffords on *Broken Arrow*, Valerie Allen, and Dick Jones. L.Q. Jones appeared in it under the credit, Justus McQueen, and Moore also took a role.

It was the story of a greedy woman and two brothers. She can't seduce Jim (Jeffords) to marry her so she can gain his money so she marries Norm

(Dick Jones). He's greedy, too. It's a grisly story with avarice leading to death. The film is almost impossible to find.

Valerie Allen and Dick Jones share an intense scene on a lobby card from the film, *The Devil's Bedroom*. (Photo credit: Courtesy of L.Q. Jones)

L.Q. Jones himself told me there are very few copies out there and calls *The Devil's Bedroom*, "possibly the world's worst picture," but he adds that it was mentioned on some of the Top 10 pictures of the year lists for 1964 and says sometimes he almost gets in fights when he calls it bad picture.

Bad or good, getting it recorded on film involved challenges including, according to the director, "The entire budget was less than studios use for paperclips. Lighting was done with household light. Film we just shot exploded out of the camera."

L.Q. Jones joked that Dick got involved because he was insane, but the reality was that Dick and Alvy Moore were good friends and the job sounded interesting to Dick at the time.

Dick remembered:

I got billing on The Devil's Bedroom. *The only thing I remember about that is that the working conditions weren't the best because it was low, low, low, cheaper than cheap budget. We did it in some little town outside of McKinney, Texas.* [Actually, it was filmed around Jacksonville, Texas.] *That's the first time I got back to McKinney, where I lived before I came out to California.*

We did a lot of night shots. One of the producers was the cameraman. He had the cheapest camera—probably got at Sam's Camera Store—a wind-up toy. A couple of times he'd say, "I gotta check the film," and he'd open up the case and the stuff would just spill out of the thing. It wasn't on the sprockets.

L.Q. Jones told the author that he was going to write a book about the filming called *The Pig Got Sick and the Horse Ran Away*. He added, "Yes, the pig got sick and we didn't have a horse."

In our interview, he praised the contribution Dick made to the filming.

Dick did whale of a job with the part he did. It went totally against Dick's grain. In the picture, he plays a crooked brother, grasping for money and run by his wife. It was a tough part. He did it marvelously well.

Dick is a very special person, so good at so many things. He was help all the way through the show. Able to help at every turn. Dick was the most experienced of anyone in cast or crew.

The outstanding memory for Dick in *The Devil's Bedroom* was rigging and doing the fire stunt.

I doubled John Lupton in the fire scene when he got cornered when the dogs and the people chased him. He was a murderer or something like that. They cornered him in this cave and wanted to set him on fire.

Lupton said, "Not on your life am I going to do that."

I made myself a fire suit out of asbestos from a pajama pattern and used that under my clothes I was using doubling him, and got my rubber cement timed out so it would burn for thirty-five, forty seconds at the most. They got all set.

They said, "We're going to be protecting you real great. We've got some water hoses here and all this water ready for you.

I said, "You put water anywhere near the scene and you're not gonna get me to do it because I don't want to be parboiled. You use dry extinguishers but it should be out. The next best thing is to throw a blanket over me and stomp on me."

That worked out real good. It photographed well, too.

L. Q. Jones also commented on the fire stunt. He talked about the riskiness of working with fire and said they were filming in a more humid atmosphere than is optimum for that work. He pointed out that the key problem in a fire stunt is "how do you breathe?" Even when all the rigging is done carefully "you strike the match" and hope all goes well, especially as Dick had rigged the burn to envelop the body in fire.

**A still of Dick doing the fire stunt he rigged for *The Devil's Bedroom*.
(Photo credit: Courtesy of L. Q. Jones)**

"The only spectacular thing in the film is the fire stunt," he said. "That's what Dick set up. It worked masterfully. Dick was a superb stuntman."

Dick's last feature film appearance was an uncredited role in the Sci-Fi cult favorite, *A Boy and His Dog*, based on the highly acclaimed novel by

Harlan Ellison. L.Q. Jones wrote and directed; Dick's friend Alvy Moore was a producer.

In the post-apocalyptical film, Dick has an uncredited cameo as the shotgun-bearing "ticket-taker" at a drive-in. He halts Don Johnson and his dog as they enter and admits them after being presented with a can of peaches.

It's a multi-layered, award-winning film with a core of devoted fans.

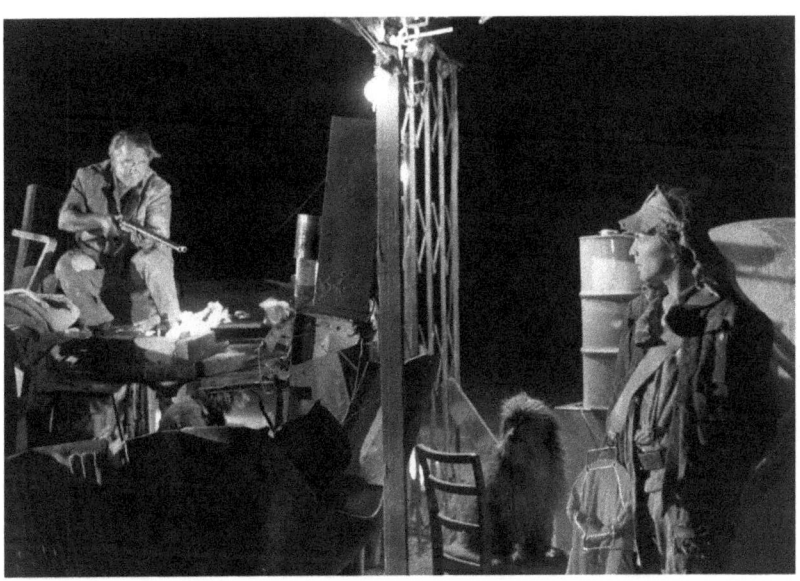

The ticket-taker (Dick Jones) holds a shotgun on Vic (Don Johnson) demanding an admission fee. (Photo credit: Courtesy of L.Q. Jones)

The film wasn't exactly Dick's cup of tea.

A Boy and His Dog. I read the story. I read the book. I worked in the picture. They tried to explain it to me. I saw it. And I still don't understand it. I saw it again and I still don't understand it. I'm not listed. I made that part of my contract with Alvy Moore and L.Q. Jones. I said I'll work for you, but don't put my name on it.

The part I had could have been done in about five minutes, but I was on that thing almost two weeks. They had an outdoor movie show, and the price of admission was a can of food, and somebody gave me a can, and I said, "I can't read it." He said, "It's canned peaches," and I looked at it again and said, "Canned peaches? Okay, come on." Or something like that. I was the ticket taker.

No matter how minimal a part Dick viewed this role, L.Q. Jones had nothing but praise for Dick's contribution.

Dick has so much talent. He's been in the business so long he had what was needed on the screen for A Boy and His Dog. *He did it and did it well, as he always does.*

You always appreciate someone like Dick who has talent and experience.

Did You Know...?

Dick Jones was not one to boast about himself. At events for which he was a guest, it was usually necessary for a panel moderator or a fan to ask specifically in order to elicit a story about his experiences.

It was the same in gathering information for this book. No way I could say, "Tell me about a particular film. Occasionally, the title would bring forth a tale, but more often a response such as, "I worked on it," would come from his lips.

Because of this, it was difficult to learn new information without having an idea of the type of incident that occurred.

One of those nuggets came to me in a roundabout way as we were working on details. In the May/June 2013 issue (#113) of *Western Clippings*, Johnny Western wrote a column concerning Robert Fuller, actor, stunt fighter, star of television series and films, and all-around nice guy. In that commentary, Western commented that Fuller and Dick Jones went through a stage when they had more of their share of real-life bar fights.

I happened to see Fuller shortly after the publication and asked him. He freely admitted his own part but denied Dick's complicity in the frays. "That was my friend Chuck Courtney," he assured me.

Wrong. Fuller and Dick may not have torn up any bars in tandem, but Dick claimed his share.

Johnny Western blows the whistle on everybody. But it was only when all the rodeo cowboys came to town. Rodeo cowboys didn't like moving picture cowboys. When you were identified as in the movies by them, the dance was on.

Dick rode rodeo in the mid-1950s. I found that out when I flew to California to get pictures from Dick's still collection. He had a number of photos of himself riding bareback broncs.

One of Dick's photos of him displaying his bronc riding skills.

Did You Know...?

From watching Dick's performances on screen, it is plain that he handled guns well, but he also explained it well. Joe Bodrie, who represented Colt guns for some years, requested that Dick teach him some gun spinning.

Dick Jones demonstrating gun spinning to Joe Bodrie in his living room. Note the framed still of Dick and Spot from *Rocky Mountain* hanging over the fireplace and the boots on the mantle. That picture hung in the Jones house as long as Dick lived—a memory of his favorite film. The boots were the ones he wore in *Trail of the Hawk* in 1935.

Dick received a number of honors recognizing his contributions to the movie industry over the years. He was among the original 1,500 celebrities to be honored with his own star on Hollywood Boulevard's Walk of Fame for his contribution to the motion picture and television industry.

One day he commented to me:

I got a surprise—a feather in my cap. I got a letter from the Hollywood Walk of Fame Committee inviting me to their Hollywood Walk of Fame honoree dinner or something to be held at the Kodak Theater on Hollywood Boulevard and they want to do it with the Red Carpet presentation coming up to the theater, and after the ceremonies have everybody brought up on the stage and take a big group photo of the ones that are still alive that are in the Hollywood Walk of Fame.

They're honoring me, and I'm very honored and surprised they would look back that far, but at least my star's still there. I don't know how I'm going to handle that. Anyway, it was nice to get the letter and I felt honored.

The thing that tickles the hell out of me is that I didn't pay for mine. They gave it to me, and I was one of the first 1,500 stuck in Hollywood Boulevard. I'm way down at the end, but it's still on Hollywood Boulevard.

Dick's star as shown on the plaque he was given when his star was laid.

Did You Know...?

I think stars started off at $15,000, then it went up to $20,000, then $25,000, and now it's $35,000 to get your star on Hollywood Boulevard. There's a lot of people who have their stars on there that they got their fan clubs to foot the bill. Lot of people wish they had one. I know a lot of people that got turned down.

Although Dick and I did not have the chance to see his star together, he did like to show it off.

My star on the Walk of Fame is at the Roosevelt Hotel. It's smack dab in front of the liquor store by the Roosevelt Hotel.

I remember one time I had two of the grandsons. I said to them, "You ever been down Hollywood Boulevard? I'll take you to see all the sights." I pointed out Grauman's Chinese, went down half-block, turned around and came back and said, "Let's go get a hot fudge sundae at the ice cream parlor. We came out, walked around in front of the hotel, and looked at my star. Kevin says, "Wow! That's YOU!" They were impressed.

Dick with his Golden Boot Award.

In 1989, Dick was presented a Golden Boot Award. That award came from his peers in the Western entertainment industry. Pat Buttram came up with the idea of honoring people who were part of cowboy movies. Buttram presented Bob Steele with a belt buckle with a Golden Boot on it at a dinner in the early 1980s. In 1983, the first Golden Boot Awards were presented to twenty-five of those instrumental in creating the cowboy film as we knew it, including Steele, Roy Rogers and Dale Evans, Gene Autry, the original Durango Kid—Charles Starrett, and stuntman Al Wyatt. Dick received his at the seventh annual ceremony.

In 1988, Dick was made an honorary member of the Hollywood Stuntmen's Hall of Fame for his outstanding stunt performances in motion pictures and television. Throughout his film career, Dick had performed his own stunts. His first screen appearance was uncredited stunts when he flew across the sound stage on wires in *Wonder Bar*. During his childhood, he was hired for many roles because he could ride a horse and do his own riding. Some of the stunts he did he would not be allowed to do now because of his young age, but he did them then.

As he got older, he did some stunts for others when the situation warranted it, as in *The Devil's Bedroom,* when he doubled John Lupton for the fire gag, and in *The Range Rider* episode, "Indian War Party," when he doubled Rodd Redwing for the fight with Jocko Mahoney.

Dick was very proud of his stunt work—deservedly. He was skilled in that area. Many have not realized just how good he was.

October 2000, Dick became a Disney Legend, receiving the Disney Legends Award during a Legends Award ceremony at Walt Disney's Studio. The Legends program recognizes the people behind the dream that made the Disney Magic. Dick received the honor for voicing Pinocchio the same year his co-star Cliff Edwards was honored posthumously as the voice of Jiminy Cricket.

The Silver Spur Award from the Reel Cowboys came to Dick in 2008. The award is given to the cowboys who rode the silver screen.

Dick's Silver Spur Award that hung on the wall of his den.

Dick has been honored in a variety of ways over the years for his film career. In Sedona, Arizona, his picture is on one of the plaques placed around the town honoring those who made films there.

He appeared in *The Strawberry Roan*, which was made in Sedona in 1948. He remembered:

We were staying in a motel, and the way it was laid out when we'd come in after work covered with this red sand we come in the back of the motel and run through the motel and wash ourselves off at a porch in the front which overlooked

Red Rock Creek, and we dive into the creek and wash off the rest of the sand. Then, we'd go back into the motel and dress and go to dinner.

Dick was handy around boats—think back to his stories of leaving the set to visit the ships in the back lot—and loved to deep sea fish.

The kind of fishing I like is long-range fishing. Get on the boat at San Diego and go 1,200 miles southwest of that and then 600 miles off the coast of Mexico. There're three islands out there. They cover about 300 miles from the farthest one out to the closest one in. That's where all the big yellow-fin tuna are. The shortest is a twelve-day trip, and the longest is an eighteen-day trip. That's my type of cruise. I don't like a "cruise" ship. Party and eat all the time. When I go fishing, I want to go fishing—twenty out of twenty-four hours a day. You have to have at least four hours of sleep.

Dick sent me a picture from one of his fishing excursions.

The information in Dick's handwriting on the back of this picture reads: Dick Jones; Friday, January 27, 1995; Clarion Island, Mexico; Boat: Royal Polaris of San Diego, California; 164.6 LB, Yellowfin Tuna.

Did You Know…?

Dick did his share of boat racing, too. One of the favorite stories requested on this topic we called, "Roy Rogers Doesn't Like to Lose."

When I was racing boats with Roy Rogers, he had bought a boat company called Yellowjacket—Yellowjacket Boat Company. A real nice runabout boat made out of molded plywood.

He started racing them. He had two 55-horsepower counter-rotated outboard engines on it with top water props. He would take it up on top of the water and just streak. It went 60 miles per hour.

He got a new boat and said, "Would you like to try it? We'll race together."

I said, "Sure, I'd like to do that."

So, he said, "You take this boat and get comfortable on it."

I took it down to the harbor and was running it around getting familiar with it, learning what I could do and what I couldn't do.

The first race I was ever in was from Cabrina Beach—Long Beach—to Catalina Island, stay over a night and come back the next morning. The race didn't end until we got back into Los Angeles Harbor.

I got my buddy, who was an ex-sailor in the war, and told him, "You'll enjoy riding around in this fast little boat." It's twenty-seven miles from Los Angeles to Avalon, where boats come in Catalina at the casino.

The night before, they had the Coast Guard give instructions on the weather and the tides. I practically went to sleep. I thought, Hell, this little boat sits on top of the water. It doesn't worry about tides. The only thing that's maybe going to affect it is maybe the weather, fog or rain. Rain doesn't bother me. Fog—I've got a whale of a good compass. I got a compass out of a tank that was real slow moving because those little boats bounce around so much you couldn't steer straight course with a regular compass. It was a big one, so I put it between my legs, under the steering wheel, away from the throttles that I had to work constantly. But I could still see that compass so I was confident there.

Anyway, I got my course and decided I'm going to go right straight for Avalon. I'm not going to worry about drift, tide or anything like that. I'm going straight for Avalon.

They all said, "You steer fifty degrees this way and that'll compensate for the tide."

The gun went off and with these top-water props you have to work at it to get the boat on plane. The boat won't go any faster than just chug, chug, chug, chug until you get on plane. So, I got my co-pilot to get up on the bow and bounce the bow of it so it would get it down and then it would go.

When the gun went off I started up. I learned later on that I could've started before the gun went off. That put me way behind the pack.

He's up there bouncing the bow of the boat to try to get it down and he falls off. So, I've got to go around and pick him up and then finally get the bow down and now she's going. We get her up there and get outside the breakwater and we see all the other boats with their rooster tails wa-a-ay out. We could barely see them because they were so far ahead of us.

I said, "We'll catch 'em." Sure enough, we got this thing going and we're doing 55, 60 miles an hour on top of the water, jumping from one wave to the other wave and just sailing along, and all of a sudden the fog came in.

We saw the others heading north, the direction the Coast Guard gave them.

My co-pilot said, "Come on. They're going that way."

I said, "No. We're going to go this way."

He said, "They're going that way. We've got to go that way or we're gonna get lost."

The year before, the fog came in, and everybody went too far south and they missed Catalina Island. They just kept on going until they ran out of gas. It was two or three days before they found all the different boats.

We're just flying. Everything is running so smooth that I even hate to even think about slowing down. I had shoved the throttles all the way forward and almost through the bulkhead.

My co-pilot got so excited and so upset. I said, "Look. Fifteen minutes more. If we don't pick up the Island in fifteen minutes, I'll go ninety degrees this way and go find the others." That calmed him down.

I no sooner said that than the fog parted and just as if I had a gun sight on the casino, the bow ring on the boat sighted right down. Dead center of the bow ring was the casino.

We pulled in there at Roy's big boat, which was the finish line, and Dale was sitting up there and called out, "You're the first ones here. Where are the others?"

I said, "They're all the way up at the other end of the island. They'll be down here in about a half-hour."

Sure enough, the whole bunch of them came down. They went all the way up the isthmus and all the way back down because they did what the Coast Guard told them to do—steer this course. Little bitty boats on top of the water don't worry about the tide.

Anyway, we're there, and Roy was upset. He said, "Boy! You were really flying. You did all right."

I said, "What do we do now?"

He said, "Well, get a good night's sleep because we've got to race back."

I said, "Should I do anything to the boat?" I'm new at this thing. I'm asking him questions.

He said, "It was running okay when you got here."

I said, "Well, what about the oil and gas?"

He said, "You've got enough to get back, don't you?"

I said, "I don't know."

He said, "Two tanks?"

Anyway, he conned me into not refueling.

The next morning, the same thing happened again. The rockets went off. The gun went off and I started up and my co-pilot gets out on the bow and starts bouncing and he falls off again. I come back around, pick him up and we get it going. They're so far out in front we couldn't see 'em.

We get going and we're just flying and we go through that pack of boats—about fifty of them—zoom, zoom, zoom, zoom. We didn't even see them after fifteen minutes on the water. We're just flying, going down swells and having a ball. Beautiful!

Got down to the harbor, just crossing L.A. Harbor to go down to the finish line, Cabrina Beach, and chup, chup, chup. It dies! The tanks are absolutely empty.

Dry! Ran out of gas just before we crossed the line. We got the paddles out; we're paddling, and here comes Roy in this Yellowjacket II. He goes flying by and yells, "Get a horse!"

That was my first experience with him. He thought that was funny that I listened to him and ran out of gas.

He said, "Dummy, you should top off your tanks to be sure."

I said, "I will the next time."

Another time, we went round and round we were so close together. It was three laps around San Diego Harbor, closed course. I got the jump on him because on the last lap around there was this great big huge aircraft carrier docked on the naval side of San Diego Harbor and when I went by it the first two times I saw how far away from the dock it was. I got as close to it as I could because there were no waves there. I'm just skimming across the top of the water.

My boat was thirteen feet. His was fifteen feet with a 65-horsepower engine, and all I had was 55. He had more power than I did, but I out-maneuvered him. I got the jump on Roy by going up the slip alongside the aircraft carrier. The last lap around I came over and swung way over. I was still alongside of him, but I went between the aircraft carrier and the dock and just sailed. I came out of that thing like I was shot out of a pop gun. I was one or two feet ahead of him. We came close together and were heading for the finish line and my bow was dragging and I couldn't get it up high enough to skip the water.

All the weight was forward because the gas had been used up, so I climbed out over the back end of the thing and am hanging on the back of the two engines. My co-pilot is driving the thing. I'm leaning back as far as I can and pulling on the engines to raise the bow of the boat up.

He still beat me. If I'd have won that one he would have been all over me because Roy sure does hate to lose. It was fun.

We had a lot of experiences boat racing.

I remember one time we had a closed-course race in the harbor at L.A. I hit a wave and went airborne about thirty or forty feet, and when you're up out of the water, there's no way of steering the boat, and there's a dead head—half-submerged log—and I plowed right into it and punched a hole in the bow of the boat. Water *just came gushing in so I pulled the plugs in the back end of the boat so the water would go on through and I knew if I ever slowed down—if I lost power—I'd lose the whole boat. Blub, blub, blub and it would go to the bottom of the bay there.*

So, I turned it around—still on plane—and I'm going back against the pack coming in. I guess they all realized that I was crazy or in trouble or something but they opened up and spread apart so that I could get through and I went all the way back to the beginning of the race and went to the docks before it started dropping. And I throttled back, shoved it forward real fast, and made the boat jump and jumped it on top of the dock so it wouldn't sink. It took me almost a month to get that thing repaired but I saved the boat.

Loving the water as he did, Dick dealt with sailboats, too.

I worked my fanny off crewing on the Queen Mab, *which was a schooner, a race boat. I crewed on that thing and crewed on it and worked more times getting it tuned up for the Trans Pac race from Los Angeles to Hawaii and the two times they asked me to go as crew I had to go on a job and both of them were locations and I was out of town and couldn't go.*

I got in one race with them and that was a little short tune-up race to Ensenada and back. I was the bow man and I'd go ride on the bowsprit and pop the spinnaker. No sooner pop the spinnaker and that would plow the bow down and I would get soaking wet. Water up to my nose. But it was fun.

One of the roles Dick would have liked to play in his Dickie Jones years was that of a regular kid in school. He mentioned the fact to me more than once.

On the set of The Kid Comes Back, *I remember the school teacher more than anything else. She was always on my case. Mrs. Horn. The main problem for them about schooling on the set was that they couldn't find me. I had to have three hours of schooling, one hour of recreation, one hour for lunch. So, technically, they only had me for three hours of filming. There was a lot of leeway there.*

Lillian Horn was the teacher at Warner Bros. for so long. She was the resident teacher at Warner Bros. She's the one that told me that if I worked days I was under her supervision, it would've amounted to a five-year contract at Warner Bros. That's how much I did at Warner. A LOT!

I didn't like working because it kept me away from school. Then, I'd go back and the other kids couldn't figure out how I could be gone so long and be right up with them. Before I'd go to work on a show, I'd get my assignments. They'd go to the school and tell them why I was going to be gone and they'd give me the work and I'd get it done and be up with the class and they couldn't figure out how I did it. I wanted to be just a regular kid without all this fol-de-rol.

The time I broke my leg and had to go to a professional school because I couldn't navigate the stairs at L.A. High, I found out what a bunch of phonies those kids were. I couldn't stand that. It was around 1941, before the war started.

That broken leg cost him the chance of an on-screen dance with Ginger Rogers. In *The Major and the Minor,* Dick was scheduled for a dancing part. At that time, he was playing school football and broke his leg. Another actor replaced him in the role. Watching the film, it is easy to identify the dance number that would have been Dick's.

In many ways, Dick was an old-fashioned kind of guy. One of those was his resistance to technology. In spite of the fact he drove wherever he wanted in the Los Angeles area, he refused a cell phone. I encouraged him to think of a minimal one in the name of safety in case of trouble, but he turned a deaf ear. When he retired, he gave away the computer and its accessories and went back to pen and ink. As a result, he missed all the Internet-related misinformation concerning him that floated around.

One thing he did hear that annoyed him but not enough to make a big fuss about it was the source of the name of his older daughter, Melody. More than once, I've seen the trivia answer that she was named after Gene Autry's Melody Ranch. Not so, said Dick, wanting to set the record straight in my notes and mind.

Back when *Along Came Jones* came out in the mid-1940s, before there was a Melody Ranch, Dick was sitting in a theater watching Gary Cooper in the film. Cooper's character's name was Melody Jones, and Dick thought to himself he liked that blend. His name was Jones and he told me that he decided at that moment that if he had a daughter, he would name her Melody

Jones. So, his daughter was named not after Autry's ranch but after Gary Cooper's character. He wanted to set that straight when we did this book, so I'm doing it for him.

Tying It Up

THERE WILL NOT BE A DEEP, DEFINITIVE BIOGRAPHY of Dick "Dickie" Jones, not from this author, anyway. That's chiefly for the reason that Dick did not want that. He was very private and wanted to share only certain parts of his life.

Before we started interviews toward a book, I asked Dick to write a short bio for me. This is what he sent:

DICK JONES
<u>BIOGRAPHY</u>

Dick Jones was born in 1927, in the small west Texas town of Snyder just south of Abilene and west of Dallas. He learned to ride about the same time he took up walking. At the age of four years, he began his career by appearing in rodeos as the "World's Youngest Trick Rider and Trick Roper."

In 1932, cowboy movie star, Hoot Gibson, was the headline attraction at the Dallas Texas State Fair, where he "discovered" little Dickie. Hoot, right away, prompted Dickie's mother into putting the boy into the movies. A few days later, the world's youngest professional cowboy, accompanied by his mother and Hoot's manager, headed for the wide open spaces of Hollywood.

Dickie earned his first movie paycheck doing stunt work in the Warner Bros. picture, Wonder Bar, starring Al Jolson. He then went on to play kid roles of all types of dramatic as well as western pictures at various studios. He probably played more star-as-a-child roles than anyone in the movie industry. He also worked with practically every cowboy actor in the business, except for some odd reason, he never worked with his mentor, Hoot Gibson.

Midyear 1938, eleven-year-old Dickie was chosen by the late Walt Disney to be the voice of Pinocchio in the animated film classic of the little wooden puppet. Between Pinocchio recording, which took place over a nineteen-month span, Dickie completed roles in a half-dozen other films.

At age fifteen, Dick went to New York for two and a half years to play the lead part of Henry Aldrich on the nationally acclaimed radio show, The Aldrich Family. Dick's part as Henry was cut short due to World War II, in which he served a two-year hitch working for Uncle Sam as a rifleman in the Army, stationed in Alaska. Upon his discharge from the service, Dick returned to Hollywood to resume his acting career.

It was in 1948 that Gene Autry hired Dick for a role in his color feature film, Strawberry Roan. Dick subsequently worked in six [sic] other Gene Autry films plus numerous TV shows of Gene's.

The latter part of 1950, upon completing the filming of Rocky Mountain, starring Errol Flynn, for Warner Bros. Studio, Gene Autry signed Dick to be the sidekick of Jock O'Mahoney in the television series, The Range Rider.

Dick's popularity in The Range Rider series prompted Autry to create a new series in which Dick would be the star, and he developed the Buffalo Bill, Jr. TV show. The TV series aired in the mid-50s with Milky Way Mars candy as the show's national sponsor.

Dick's motion picture, radio, and television career spans fifty-five years. He has appeared in nearly 100 movies and over 200 television productions. He was among the original 1,500 celebrities to be honored with his own star on Hollywood Boulevard's Walk of Fame for his contribution to the motion picture and television industry. In 1989, Dick was presented the prestigious Golden Boot Award by his peers in the Western entertainment industry. In 1988, he was inducted into the Hollywood Stuntmen's Hall of Fame for his outstanding stunt performances in motion pictures and television. October 2000, Dick was the recipient of the Disney Legends Award, presented to him during the Legends Award ceremony at Walt Disney's Studio by Michael Eisner, C.E.O., and Roy E. Disney.

Notice that the "bio" is basically a resume. Nothing about family. Nothing truly personal. That is precisely what he wanted to share, and I worked to follow his wishes.

The author with Dick Jones and his only permanent string, his wife Betty, a dear and delightful woman. Family meant everything to Dick.

Dick told me, "I use the adage, Gene (Autry) has the Midas touch. Everything he touched turned to gold—everything except me."

Autry may not have been the springboard for a skyrocketing career in film for Dick, but in the long run, Dick had the kind of wealth that doesn't come from film fame. Dick and Betty were married more than sixty-five years.

They had children and grandchildren who loved them deeply and gathered with them for occasions and just to visit. I have year after year of multi-generation Christmas card photos with happy, smiling faces, and can recall a few stories Dick told about the kids and grandkids that were *not* for publication.

Dick Jones was his own man. No strings? No. There were not. Dick was a good man and a caring man. He believed in what he believed in and no amount of pressure swayed him from where he stood. It was a joy to know Dick and Betty. I consider myself blessed.

Annotated Filmography

(Note: When Dick Jones was billed in the top five cast names, his name is included in the cast credits.)

1934

Wonder Bar. First National Pictures. Director: Lloyd Bacon.
Al Jolson, Kay Francis, Dolores Del Rio, Guy Kibbee, Dick Powell.
Storyline note: Musical drama set in Paris with Busby Berkeley production numbers.
Dick's role: aerial stunts.

Life of Vergie Winters, The. RKO Radio Pictures. Director: Alfred Santell.
Ann Harding, John Boles, Helen Vinson.
Storyline note: John Boles has a promising political career but his love for Ann Harding causes gossip that could bring them both down.
Dick's role: unknown child role.

Fifteen Wives. Invincible Films. Director: Frank R. Strayer.
Natalie Moorhead, Conway Tearle, Almeda Fowler, Raymond Hatton, Margaret Dumont.
Storyline note: When a man found dead of apparent natural causes turns out to have had fifteen wives, any good detective might suspect murder. It's a good bet one of the fifteen killed him, but which one?
Dick's role: unknown child role.

Now and Forever. Paramount Pictures. Director: Henry Hathaway.
Carole Lombard, Gary Cooper, Shirley Temple, Sir Guy Standing.
Storyline note: Carefree Gary Cooper's irresponsibility irritates his wife. Can the addition of his perky young daughter to their lives turn him around?
Dick's role: extra in party scene.

Kid Millions. Samuel Goldwyn Studios. Director: Roy Del Ruth.
Eddie Cantor, Ethel Merman, Ann Sothern, George Murphy.
Storyline note: Music and comedy dominate as Eddie Cantor inherits $77 million from his uncle, a happening that starts rather than ends his comic troubles.
Dick's role: Little boy in ice cream number.

Babes in Toyland. (Video title: *March of the Wooden Soldiers*). Hal Roach Pictures. Director: Gus Meins.
Stan Laurel, Oliver Hardy, Henry Brandon.
Storyline note: Laurel and Hardy version of the Victor Herbert operetta.
Dick's role: Schoolboy.

Strange Wives. Universal. Director: Richard Thorpe.
Ester Ralston, Roger Pryor, June Clayworth, Hugh O'Connell, Cesar Romero.
Storyline note: Roger Pryor marries a Russian woman only to discover that the saying one marries the spouse's family is too, too true.
Dick's role: Twin.

Little Men. Mascot Pictures. Director: Phil Rosen.
Ralph Morgan, Erin O'Brien-Moore, Frankie Darro.
Storyline note: Early film version of the Louisa May Alcott novel about Jo March Bhaer and her husband Fritz who run a school for boys.
Dick's role: Dolly.

Burn 'Em Up Barnes. Mascot Pictures. 12-chapter serial. Directors: Colbert Clark, Armand Schaefer.
Jack Mulhall, Frankie Darro, Lola Lane, Jason Robards, Sr., Julian Rivero.
Storyline note: Race-car driver Jack Mulhall, his adopted ward Frankie Darro in tow, comes to the rescue of Lola Lane, whose apparently worthless property holds oil that villain Jason Robards, Sr. is out to get.
Dick's role: Schoolboy.

1935

Queen of the Jungle. Chadwick Productions (Universal Studios). Herman Wohl Productions. Director: Robert F. Hill.
Mary Kornman, Reed Howes, Lafe McKee.
Storyline note: Twelve-chapter serial with all of the standard jungle adventure elements.
Dick's role: David Worth, Jr. as a boy.

Call of the Savage. Universal. 12 chapter serial. Director: Lew Landers.
Noah Beery, Jr., Harry Woods, Walter Miller, Dorothy Short.

Storyline note: Competition between two teams of scientists adds a slightly different twist to this serial set in the African jungle.

Dick's role: Jan Trevor as a boy.

Trail of the Hawk aka *The Hawk*. Affiliated Pictures. Director: Edward Dmytryk.

Yancey Lane, Betty Jordan, Dickie Jones, Lafe McKee, Rollo Dix.

Storyline note: A boy's dying mother tells him of his true identity. It's a complicated trail to prove it and claim his inheritance.

Dick's role: Dickie Thomas.

Westward Ho. Republic. Director: Robert N. Bradbury.

John Wayne, Sheila Mannors, Jack Curtis, Yakima Canutt, Hank Bell, Glenn Strange, Earl Dwire.

Storyline note: A gang attacks wagons going West. Two young brothers survive the attack. One is kidnapped by the gang. As adults, the brothers meet again, one brother out to avenge the murder of his parents, the other brother now part of the gang.

Dick's role: Jim Wyatt as a boy.

Moonlight on the Prairie. Warner Bros. Director: D. Ross Lederman.

Dick Foran, Sheila Mannors, George E. Stone, Gordon "Wild Bill" Elliott, Bud Osborne.

Storyline note: Dick Foran has been falsely accused of murder. He aligns himself with the murdered man's widow to find the real killer.

Dick's role: Dickie Roberts.

Our Gang Follies of 1936. Hal Roach Pictures. *Our Gang* Series. Director: Gus Meins.

George "Spanky" McFarland, Darla Hood, Carl "Alfalfa" Switzer, Billie "Buckwheat" Thomas, Eugene "Porky" Lee.

Storyline note: The gang is putting on a show but the Flory Dory Sixtet, the featured performers, don't show. Something has to be done and Spanky's just the boy to do it.

Dick's role: Dickie; also in Spanky's chorus line.

1936

Gasoloons. RKO. One-reel short. Director: Arthur Ripley.

Edgar Kennedy, Florence Lake, Dot Farley, Jack Rice.

Storyline note: A family notices the station where they stop for gas is for sale and they decide to buy it and run it.

Dick's role: Wilbur.

The Pinch Singer. Hal Roach Pictures. *Our Gang* series. Director: Fred C. Newmeyer.

George "Spanky" McFarland, Darla Hood, Carl "Alfalfa" Switzer, Billie "Buckwheat" Thomas.

Storyline note: The gang holds auditions among themselves to see who will represent them in the radio station contest. Darla wins but runs late and Alfalfa becomes the "pinch" singer.

Dick's role: Dance chorus in contest.

Sutter's Gold. Universal. Director: James Cruze.

Edward Arnold, Lee Tracy, Binnie Barnes, Addison Richards, Harry Carey, Sr.

Storyline note: Biopic of the man upon whose land was the gold strike that started the California Gold Rush.

Dick's role: Second newsboy.

Adventures of Frank Merriwell. Universal. 12 chapter serial. Director: Cliff Smith.

Don Briggs, Jean Rogers, John "Dusty" King, House Peters, Jr.

Storyline note: Based on a series of 19th century books, college athlete Frank Merriwell (Don Briggs) not only has exciting adventures but also arrives back on campus in time to win the game.

Dick's role: Jimmy McLaw.

Exclusive Story. MGM. Director: George B. Seitz.

Joseph Calleria, Franchot Tone, Madge Evans, J. Farrell MacDonald.

Storyline note: Franchot Tone is the lawyer for a newspaper trying to get the goods on crime boss Joseph Calleria.

Dick's role: Higgins' son.

Wife vs. Secretary. MGM. Director: Clarence Brown.

Clark Gable, Jean Harlow, James Stewart, Myrna Loy.

Storyline note: Jean Harlow is Clark Gable's super-efficient secretary but wife Myrna Loy suspects she is much more.

Dick's role: unnamed little brother of Harlow.

The First Baby. Fox. Director: Lewis Seiler.

Johnny Downs, Shirley Deane, Jane Darwell, Ward Bond, Gene Lockhart, Hattie McDaniel.

Storyline note: When the first baby arrives a mother-in-law's dominating ways disrupt a marriage. She has learned her lesson by the time the couple has its second child.

Dick's role: Ellis child.

Who's Looney Now. RKO. One-reel short. Director: Leslie Goodwins.

Jack Norton, Vivien Oakland, Billy Gilbert, Tempe Pigott.

Storyline note: Jack Norton tries to follow a friend's advice on how to get his wild family under control.

Dick's role: Sonny Brown.

Daniel Boone. RKO. Director: David Howard.

George O'Brien, Heather Angel, John Carradine, Clarence Muse, Ralph Forbes.

Storyline note: George O'Brien is historical figure Daniel Boone, settling Kentucky against all odds.

Dick's role: Master Jerry Randolph.

Wild Horse Round-Up. Ambassador Pictures. Director: Alan James.

Kermit Maynard, Betty Lloyd (Beth Marion), Dickie Jones, Dick Curtis, John Merton.

Storyline note: Kermit Maynard fights a land grab scheme and courts Betty Lloyd.

Dick's role: Dickie Williams.

1937

Black Legion. Warner Bros. Director: Archie Mayo.

Humphrey Bogart, Erin O'Brien-Moore, Anne Sheridan, Dick Foran.

Storyline note: Humphrey Bogart becomes involved in a xenophobic secret society with dire results.

Dick's role: Buddy Taylor.

Blake of Scotland Yard. Victory Pictures (Sam Katzman). 15 chapter serial. Director: Robert F. Hill.

Ralph Byrd, Joan Barclay, Herbert Rawlinson, Lloyd Hughes, Dickie Jones.

Storyline note: Blake's adversary in this action-packed serial is the Scorpion, who seeks control of a death ray machine.

Dick's role: Bobby Mason.

Land Beyond the Law. Warner Bros. Director: B. Reeves Eason.

Dick Foran, Linda Perry, Wayne Morris, Glenn Strange, Harry Woods, Edmund Cobb, Bud Osborne.

Storyline note: Dick Foran overcomes his rep as a wild boy to become sheriff and round up the baddies.
Dick's role: Bobby Skinner.

Smoke Tree Range. Universal. Director: Lesley Selander.
Buck Jones, Muriel Evans, John Elliott, Dickie Jones, Edmund Cobb, Charles King.
Storyline note: Buck Jones must not only fight cattle rustlers but also convince his grandfather that Muriel Evans should be able to keep her land.
Dick's role: Teddy Page.

Flying Fists. Victory Pictures (Sam Katzman). Director: Robert F. Hill.
Herman Brix (Bruce Bennett), Jeanne Martel, Fuzzy Knight, J. Farrell MacDonald, Guinn "Big Boy" Williams, William "Billy" Benedict.
Plot: A lumberjack gets caught up in the fight game.
Dick's role: Dickie Martin.

Stella Dallas. United Artists. Director: King Vidor.
Barbara Stanwyck, John Boles, Anne Shirley, Tim Holt.
Storyline note: Classic performance by Stanwyck in a soap opera tale of a small-town woman who sacrifices everything for her daughter.
Dick's role: Lee Morrison.

Renfrew of the Royal Mounties. Grand National. Director: Al Herman.
James Newill, Carol Hughes, William Royle, Kenneth Harlan, Chief Thundercloud.
Storyline note: James Newill is a Mountie on the trail of a counterfeiting ring.
Dick's role: Tommy MacDonald.

Love Is on the Air. Warner Bros. Director: Nick Grinde.
Ronald Reagan, Jane Travis, Ben Welden, Raymond Hatton, Robert Barrat, Willard Parker, Herbert Rawlinson.

Storyline note: Ronald Reagan stars as a radio personality who finds corruption among city officials but is sidetracked in his campaign against them.

Dick's role: Bill (Mouse's friend).

The Pigskin Palooka. Hal Roach Pictures. *Our Gang* series. Director: Gordon Douglas.

George "Spanky" McFarland, Darla Hood, Carl "Alfalfa" Switzer, Billie "Buckwheat" Thomas, Eugene "Porky" Lee.

Storyline note: Alfalfa brags of his football prowess in a letter and must prove it to the gang when he gets home.

Dick's role: Spike.

Hollywood Round-Up. Columbia. Director: Ewing Scott.

Buck Jones, Helen Twelvetrees, Grant Withers, Shemp Howard, Dickie Jones.

Storyline note: Buck Jones is a straight-up stuntman doubling an ego-centered star in this Western about making a Western movie. Dickie saves the day when Buck is denied the credit for rounding up the bank robbers.

Dick's role: Dickie Stevens.

Our Gang Follies of 1938. Hal Roach. *Our Gang* series. Director: Gordon Douglas.

George "Spanky" McFarland, Darla Hood, Carl "Alfalfa" Switzer, Billie "Buckwheat" Thomas, Eugene "Porky" Lee, Henry Brandon.

Storyline note: Alfalfa wants to give up crooning for opera, to the Gang's woe. A nightmare in which the gang's income for performing reaches "hundreds of thousands of dollars" makes him have second thoughts.

Dick's role: Dickie.

1938

The Kid Comes Back. Warner Bros. Director: B. Reeves Eason.
Wayne Morris, Barton McLane, Maxie Rosenbloom, Ames Robins.
Storyline note: A boxing tale with the usual girl who doesn't want her guy to fight conflicting with his desire to be a champion.
Dick's role: Bobby Doyle.

Border Wolves. Universal. Director: Joseph H. Lewis.
Bob Baker, Constance Moore, Fuzzy Knight, Dickie Jones, Glenn Strange, Hank Bell.
Storyline note: Bob Baker is falsely arrested for murder but is released by a knowing judge to bring the real gang to justice.
Dick's role: Jimmie Benton.

Land of Fighting Men. Monogram. Director: Alan James.
Jack Randall, Louise Stanley, Herman Brix (Bruce Bennett), Dickie Jones, John Merton, Lane Chandler, Rex Lease, Robert Burns.
Storyline note: Jack Randall must prove his innocence and bring in the real killer.
Dick's role: Jimmy Mitchell.

Devil's Party. Universal. Director: Ray McCarey.
Victor McLaglen, Paul Kelly, William Gargan, Beatrice Roberts, Frank Jenks, John Gallaudet, Samuel S. Hinds.
Storyline note: Former Hell's Kitchen pals become involved in murder in this melodrama.
Dick's role: Joe O'Mara as a boy.

The Great Adventures of Wild Bill Hickok. Columbia. 15 chapter serial. Directors: Mack V. Wright, Sam Nelson.
Gordon "Wild Bill" Elliott, Kermit Maynard, Dickie Jones, Monte Blue,

Chief Thundercloud, Carole Wayne, Frankie Darro, Sammy McKim, George Chesebro, Edmund Cobb, Roscoe Ates.

Storyline note: Wild Bill Hickok (Elliott) fights the Phantom Raiders with the aid of the Flaming Arrows, a group of the boys – for 15 chapters.

Dick's role: Buddy.

A Man to Remember. RKO. Director: Garson Kanin.

Edward Ellis, Anne Shirley, Lee Bowman, William Henry.

Storyline note: Story of a country doctor whose life was spent caring for those who paid him in eggs and potatoes.

Dick's role: Dick Abbott as a boy.

Girls on Probation. Warner Bros. Director: William C. McGann.

Jane Bryan, Sheila Bromley, Ronald Reagan, Henry O'Neil, Susan Hayward, Anthony Averill.

Storyline note: Poor Jane Bryan just can't seem to disentangle herself from Sheila Bromley's criminal schemes. The blame always falls on her.

Dick's role: Magazine newsboy/witness.

The Frontiersmen. Paramount. Director: Lesley Selander. Producer: Harry Sherman.

William "Hopalong Cassidy" Boyd, Evelyn Venable. Russell "Lucky" Hayden, George "Gabby" Hayes, Roy Barcroft, Blackjack Ward.

Storyline note: Hoppy's corralling rowdy kids as well as rustlers in this entry in the Hopalong Cassidy series.

Dick's role: Artie Peters.

1939

Beware, Spooks! Columbia. Director: Edward Sedgwick.

Joe E. Brown, Mary Carlisle, Marc Lawrence, George J. Lewis.

Storyline note: Bumbling detective chases criminals in amusement park haunted house.

Dick's role: First boy.

Woman Doctor. RKO Radio Pictures. Director: Sidney Salkow.

Frieda Inescort, Henry Wilcoxson, Sybil Jason.

Storyline note: A woman doctor is devoted to her career.

Dick's role: Johnny.

Nancy Drew ... Reporter. First National. Director: William Clemens.

Bonita Granville, Frankie Thomas, Jr., Dickie Jones, Mary Lee, John Litel, Jack Perry.

Storyline note: Bonita Granville is determined to produce a scoop that will win the newspaper's school reporter contest. She involves her friends and dad in helping her solve a crime in order to get her story.

Dick's role: Killer Parkins.

Sergeant Madden. MGM. Director: Josef von Sternberg.

Wallace Beery, Laraine Day, Tom Brown, Alan Curtis, Marc Lawrence.

Storyline note: Wallace Beery is a stereotypical Irish policeman whose rebellious son brings grief to the family.

Dick's role: Dennis Madden as a boy.

The Man Who Dared. Warner Bros. Director: Crane Wilbur.

Charles Grapewin, Henry O'Neil, Jane Bryan.

Storyline note: A family takes a stand against corruption in a small town.

Dick's role: William "Bill/Willie" Carter.

Young Mister Lincoln. 20th Century Fox. Director: John Ford.

Henry Fonda, Alice Brady, Eddie Quillan, Donald Meek, Marjorie Weaver.

Storyline note: Fictionalized story of Abraham Lincoln when he was a young lawyer.

Dick's role: Adam Clay as a boy.

Sky Patrol. Monogram. Director: Howard Bretherton.

John Trent, Marjorie Reynolds, Milburn Stone, Jason Robards, Jackie Coogan, John Peters, Johnny Day.

Storyline note: John Trent as Tailspin Tommy and pals his return from *Danger Flight*. In this one he's not only training young fliers but must rescue one who is shot down by the bad guys.

Dick's role: Bobbie.

Mister Smith Goes to Washington. Columbia. Director: Frank Capra.

James Stewart, Jean Arthur, Claude Rains, Guy Kibbee, Edward Arnold, Thomas Mitchell, Harry Carey, Sr.

Storyline note: Naive and honest Jefferson Smith fills a vacancy in the U.S. Senate where he finds political corruption that challenges his values.

Dick's role: Pageboy Richard Jones.

Destry Rides Again. Universal. Director: George Marshall.

James Stewart, Marlene Dietrich, Brian Donlevy, Una Merkel, Mischa Auer, Charles Winninger, Allen Jenkins, Billy Gilbert, Jack Carson, Irene Hervey, Tom Fadden, Warren Hymer.

Storyline note: The town of Bottleneck is delighted when the son of a famous lawman comes to town but the son doesn't believe that gun law is the way to go.

Dick's role: Claggett boy.

1940

Pinocchio. Walt Disney. Directors: Ben Sharpsteen, Hamilton Luske.

Voices of Cliff Edwards, Dickie Jones, Evelyn Venable, Christian Rub, Walter Catlett, Frankie Darro.

Storyline note: Disney's classic animated version of Carlo Collodi's tale of a wooden puppet who wants to be a real boy to his loving creator and "father," Gepetto.

Dick's role: The voice of Pinocchio

Virginia City. Warner Bros. Director: Michael Curtiz.

Errol Flynn, Miriam Hopkins, Randolph Scott, Humphrey Bogart, Alan Hale, Guinn "Big Boy" Williams, Frank McHugh, John Litel.

Storyline note: Civil War Western with Errol Flynn trying to stop gold from reaching the Confederacy.

Dick's role: Cobby.

Hi-Yo Silver. Republic. Directors: William Witney, John English.

Lee Powell, Herman Brix (Bruce Bennett), Chief Thundercloud, Raymond Hatton, Sammy McKim, John Merton, Lane Chandler.

Storyline note: The feature-length version of the 1938 serial, *The Lone Ranger*, was released with additional footage of Raymond Hatton telling the story to Dickie Jones.

Dick's role: The boy.

Maryland. 20th Century Fox. Director: Henry King.

Walter Brennan, Fay Bainter, John Payne, Brenda Joyce.

Storyline note: After her husband is killed in a riding accident, Fay Bainter insists that her son, John Payne, have nothing to do with horses. That only works until Brenda Joyce catches his eye and he is pulled into the equestrian world.

Dick's role: Lee Danfield, age 11.

The Howards of Virginia. Frank Lloyd Productions/Columbia. Director: Frank Lloyd.

Cary Grant, Martha Scott, Sir Cedric Hardwicke, Richard Carlson, Forrest Tucker.
Storyline note: In this story of the American Revolution Cary Grant is firmly committed to freedom while his brother-in-law is a strong royalist.
Dick's role: Matt Howard at 12.

Brigham Young. 20th Century Fox. Director: Henry Hathaway.
Dean Jagger, Tyrone Power, Linda Darnell, Brian Donlevy, John Carradine, Mary Astor, Stanley Andrews, Ann Todd.
Storyline note: Story of the Mormon leader strays from historical accuracy.
Dick's role: Henry Kent.

Knute Rockne, All American. Warner Bros. Director: Lloyd Bacon.
Pat O'Brien, Ronald Reagan, Gale Page, Donald Crisp.
Storyline note: Bio-pic of the famed Notre Dame football coach with O'Brien in the title role.
Dick's role: Boy captain.

1941

Adventure in Washington aka *Senate Pageboys*. Columbia. Director: Alfred E. Green.
Herbert Marshall, Virginia Bruce, Gene Reynolds.
Storyline note: Senator attempts to reform a wayward Senate pageboy.
Dick's role: Abbott.

1942

The Vanishing Virginian. MGM. Director: Frank Borzage.
Kathryn Grayson, Frank Morgan, Spring Byington, Natalie Thompson, Scotty Beckett, Juanita Quigley.

Storyline note: Based on an autobiographical best seller, the film tells the tale of a Virginia family moving through social changes.
Dick's role: Robert Yancey, Jr.

This Gun for Hire. Paramount. Director: Frank Tuttle.
Veronica Lake, Robert Preston, Alan Ladd, Laird Cregar, Tully Marshall, Marc Lawrence, Pamela Blake.
Storyline note: Classic crime film with Alan Ladd hired to kill for then double-crossed by Laird Cregar. Robert Preston is the cop on his tail; Veronica Lake the cop's performer girlfriend with her own agenda that catches her in the middle.
Dick's role: Raven as a boy (edited from wide-release cut).

1943

Mountain Rhythm. Republic. Director: Frank McDonald.
Weaver Brothers and Elviry.
Storyline note: The Weaver family's move puts them in conflict with a nearby boys' school.
Dick's role: Darwood Gates Alton.

Heaven Can Wait. 20th Century Fox. Director: Ernst Lubitsch.
Don Ameche, Gene Tierney, Charles Coburn, Allyn Joslyn, Laird Cregar.
Storyline note: Don Ameche dies and goes to the Devil (Laird Cregar) but the Devil doesn't want him. He's not bad enough.
Dick's role: Albert Van Cleve age 15.

The Outlaw. Howard Hughes Productions (1943). (Re-released in 1946 via RKO). Director: Howard Hughes. (Howard Hawks began the film but withdrew.)
Jane Russell, Jack Buetel, Walter Huston, Thomas Mitchell.

Storyline note: Howard Hughes' version of the Billy the Kid story but the emphasis was on Jane Russell not The Kid.

Dick's role: Boy.

1944

The Adventures of Mark Twain. Warner Bros. Director: Irving Rapper.
Fredric March, Alexis Smith, Donald Crisp, John Carradine.
Storyline note: Not wonderfully accurate but nevertheless entertaining view of the life of Mark Twain (Samuel Clemens).
Dick's role: Samuel Clemens age 15.

1948

Angel on the Amazon. Republic. Director: John H. Auer.
Vera Hruba Ralston, George Brent, Constance Bennett.
Storyline note: A woman who lives in the jungle never ages as a result of a trauma she suffered.
Dick's role: George.

Strawberry Roan. Columbia. Director: John English.
Gene Autry, Gloria Henry, Jack Holt, Dick Jones, Pat Buttram.
Storyline note: It's all about saving Champion after the horse injures young Dick Jones. Jack Holt wants to shoot him but Gene Autry knows the tamed horse can help the boy heal.
Dick's role: Joe Bailey.

1949

Battleground. MGM. Director: William Wellman.
Van Johnson, John Hodiak, Ricardo Montalban, Denise Darcel, George Murphy, Marshall Thompson, Don Taylor, Richard Jaeckel, Jerome

Courtland, Leon Ames, Douglas Fowley, James Whitmore, James Arness, Tommy Brown, Scotty Beckett.
Storyline note: Oscar-winning tale of the Battle of the Bulge has grit and realism.
Dick's role: Tanker.

Sands of Iwo Jima. Republic. Director: Allan Dwan.
John Wayne, John Agar, Forrest Tucker, Richard Jaeckel, Adele Mara.
Storyline note: Tough Marine sergeant John Wayne may not be loved by his troops but his harsh training methods pay off at the Battle of Iwo Jima. Wartime film footage helps the film to impress.
Dick's role: Scared Marine.

Missionary to Walker's Garage. Family Films.
This 28-minute, black and white film is only available on 16mm.
Storyline note: A son tries to explain to his family that he is not called to be a minister but rather a Christian businessman.
Dick's role: Mark.

Sons of New Mexico. Columbia. Director: John English.
Gene Autry, Gail Davis, Robert Armstrong, Dick Jones, Clayton Moore, Frankie Darro, Irving Bacon, Pierce Lyden.
Storyline note: It's up to Gene Autry to set his young ward, Dick Jones, on the straight and narrow and save him from his gambling cronies.
Dick's role: Randy Pryor.

1950

Military Academy with That Tenth Avenue Gang. Columbia. Director: D. Ross Lederman.
Stanley Clements, Robert Walker, Myron Wilton, Gene Collins, Leon Tyler.

Storyline note: A judge sentences four juvenile delinquents to a military school in hopes of straightening them out.
Dick's role: Richard Reilly.

Redwood Forest Trail. Republic. Director: Philip Ford.
Rex Allen, Jeff Donnell, Carl "Alfalfa" Switzer, Jane Darwell, John Cason.
Storyline note: Rex Allen comes to the rescue of a camp for underprivileged boys whose land is threatened by a lumber baron.
Dick's role: Mighty Mite.

Rocky Mountain. Warner Bros. Director: William Keighley.
Errol Flynn, Patrice Wymore, Scott Forbes, Guinn "Big Boy" Williams, Dick Jones, Buzz Henry, Slim Pickens, Sheb Wooley, Yakima Canutt.
Storyline note: Errol Flynn is trying to recruit for the Confederacy in California but the pickings are slim and conflict with Indians complicates the effort.
Dick's role: Buck "Jim" Wheat (CSA).

1951

Fort Worth. Warner Bros. Director: Edwin L. Marin.
Randolph Scott, Phyllis Thaxter, David Brian, Helene Carter, Dick Jones, Bob Steele, Kermit Maynard, Walter Sande, Ray Teal.
Storyline note: Randolph Scott hangs up his guns to become a newspaperman, but when trouble comes will words be enough to win the day?
Dick's role: Luther Wicks.

1952

The Old West. Columbia. Director: George Archainbaud.
Gene Autry, Gail Davis, Pat Buttram, Lyle Talbot, Tom London, John Merton.

Storyline note: Gene Autry links up with a parson to clean up the town of Saddlerock.

Dick's role: Pinto.

Wagon Team. Columbia. Director: George Archainbaud.

Gene Autry, Gail Davis, Pat Buttram, Dick Jones, George J. Lewis, Pierce Lyden, Gregg Barton.

Storyline note: Gene Autry goes undercover to persuade Dick Jones to give himself up and return the stolen money.

Dick's role: Dave Weldon aka The Apache Kid.

1953

Last of the Pony Riders. Columbia. Director: George Archainbaud.

Gene Autry, Kathleen Case, Dick Jones, Smiley Burnette, Gregg Barton, Buzz Henry.

Storyline note: Gene Autry fights to keep the pony riders (Pony Express) safe as the mail contracts shift to stage lines. Not only was it the last stand for the riders but also for Autry in his last theatrical feature film as a cowboy star.

Dick's role: Johnny Blair.

1954

The Bamboo Prison. Columbia. Director: Lewis Seiler.

Robert Francis, Brian Keith, Jerome Courtland, Dianne Foster, Jack Kelly, Keye Luke, Buzz Henry.

Storyline note: Story of American prisoners of war trying to escape from a Korean prison camp.

Dick's role: P.O.W. Jackie.

1956

The Wild Dakotas. Associated Film Releasing. Director: Sam Newfield.

Bill Williams, Colleen Gray, Jim Davis, John Litel, Dick Jones, John Miljan, Lisa Montell, I. Stanford Jolley, Iron Eyes Cody.

Storyline note: Conflict between settlers and Indians is agitated by a wagonmaster.

Dick's role: Mike McGeehee

1958

The Cool and the Crazy. American International/Imperial Productions. Director: William Witney.

Scott Marlow, Gigi Perreau, Dick Bakalyan, Dick Jones.

Storyline note: Teen-oriented scare tale of the evils of marijuana set smack in Middle America, Kansas City, and filmed on location in Kansas.

Dick's role: Stu Summerville.

1960

Shadow of a Boomerang. Billy Graham/World Wide Pictures. Director: Dick Ross.

Georgia Lee Hoops, Dick Jones, Jimmy Little, Billy Graham.

Storyline note: A message by evangelist Billy Graham changes the lives of Americans who have moved to a ranch in Australia.

Dick's role: Bob Prince.

1964

The Devil's Bedroom. L Q Jaff Productions/Manson Distributing. Director: L.Q. Jones.

John Lupton, Valerie Allen, Dick Jones, L.Q. Jones, Alvy Moore, Morgan Woodward.

Storyline note: Greed and betrayal move this story of a family fighting over oil riches.

Dick's role: Norm.

1965

Requiem for a Gunfighter. Paramount. Director: Spencer G. Bennet.

Rod Cameron, Stephen McNally, Mike Mazurki, Johnny Mack Brown, Tim McCoy, Bob Steele, Lane Chandler, Raymond Hatton, Rand Brooks, Edmund Cobb, Boyd "Red" Morgan, Dale Van Sickel.

Storyline note: A company of seasoned Western regulars fill the screen in this tale of a gunfighter mistaken for a judge who takes on the mantle of law and order.

Dick's role: Cliff Fletcher.

1975

A Boy and His Dog. (1976, and Dick said 1974) L Q Jaff Productions. Director: L.Q. Jones

Don Johnson, Jason Robards, L.Q. Jones, Alvy Moore.

Storyline note: Adapted from a Harlan Ellison novel, this sci-fi satire features Don Johnson as a scavenging survivor in a post-nuclear holocaust world. He is aided by his intelligent, telepathic dog.

Dick's role: Ticket taker (uncredited cameo).

Sources

THE CHIEF SOURCE WAS DICK JONES. He and I spent hours in recorded conversations, which I transcribed and edited to use. He was the source for most of the photos used, though some are ones friends and I took at events.

His wife, Betty, helped by reminding him of stories and encouraging the process. She contributed a few tales of her own.

I spent days repeatedly watching his films that I had been able to locate, and more hours searching for films in which he was reported to have appeared.

This was not a book from secondary research but from primary sources. The films are listed in the Annotated Filmography. The words from Dick are in notebooks and computer files along with the pictures. Much information about Dick, some true, some false, floats around cyberspace, but there is no list of sources to which I can send readers for further reference.

Appendix I
Categorizing the Early Films

DURING DICK'S CAREER AS A CHILD ACTOR, his roles often were of a certain type. One of those was "As a Boy." In these films, Dickie grew up to be another actor. Sometimes, he was not the only child actor to share the role, but held it for a scene or two, such as in *The Adventures of Mark Twain* and *Heaven Can Wait*. In the former, he turns into Fredric March; in the latter, Allyn Joslin.

The "As a Boy" films were:

Westward Ho, starring John Wayne. Jim Wyatt grew into Frank McGlynn, Jr.

Queen of the Jungle, starring Mary Kornman and Reed Howes. David Worth became Reed Howes.

Call of the Savage, starring Noah Beery, Jr. Jan Trevor became Noah Beery, Jr.

Stella Dallas, starring Barbara Stanwyck. Lee Morrison's adult performer was uncredited.

Devil's Party, starring Victor McLaglen. Joe O'Mara grew into John Gallaudet.

A Man to Remember, starring Edward Ellis. Dick Abbott became Lee Bowman.

Young Mister Lincoln, starring Henry Fonda. Adam Clay grew into Eddie Quillan.

Sergeant Madden, starring Wallace Beery. Dennis Madden became Alan Curtis.

Maryland, starring Walter Brennan, Fay Bainter and John Payne. It took several young actors to turn into John Payne. Dick played Lee Danfield at 11.

The Howards of Virginia, starring Cary Grant. Matt Howard would grow into Cary Grant.

This Gun for Hire, starring Veronica Lake, Robert Preston and Alan Ladd. Dick played the young Raven (Alan Ladd) in a dream sequence.

Another way to classify young Dickie's roles was as "Aw, Sis. Go on and Kiss Him." Those were most often in the mid-1930s and were Westerns. The hero comes to the rescue of young Dickie and his sister when the villains were about to steal the ranch or some other nefarious deed. The girl always finds a stumbling block to romance with the man in the white hat. Dickie is on the side of the rescuer. At times, his sister is amenable to romance but hesitant about expressing it. In a few films, Dickie actually tells the actress playing his sister to kiss the hero. All of these are great fun to watch.

The "Aw, Sis . . ." films were:

Trail of the Hawk, starring Yancey Lane and Betty Jordan.

Wild Horse Round-Up, starring Kermit Maynard and Betty Lloyd (Beth Marion).

Smoke Tree Range, starring Buck Jones and Muriel Evans.

Blake of Scotland Yard, starring Ralph Byrd, Herbert Rawlinson and Joan Barclay. Bobby Mason doesn't have to push his sister toward Jerry Sheehan but he does encourage the match.

Hollywood Round-Up, starring Buck Jones and Helen Twelvetrees.

Appendix II
Billed Together

From childhood, Dick appeared in movies with the same people. It might only be for one pairing, but often the same character actors would be on the same bill. The teamings presented here are not meant to be complete but simply some of the interesting casting connections throughout Dick's career.

Here are some of the most common "partnerships" in Dick's career starting with the juvenile actors.

As a boy, Dick appeared with other child actors. The one most often shown in cast listings was Tommy Bupp. They were billed in almost ten films together, *Babes in Toyland, Kid Millions, Little Men, Sutter's Gold, Love Is on the Air, Devil's Party, The Man Who Dared, Mister Smith Goes to Washington,* and *Beware, Spooks!*

Scotty Beckett crossed paths with Dick through five films to adulthood, *Babes in Toyland, Devil's Party, The Vanishing Virginian, Heaven Can Wait,* and *Battleground,* plus the *Our Gang* shorts.

Others often sharing credits in his early years were Buster Phelps (*Now and Forever, Strange Wives, Little Men,* and *The Howards of Virginia*) and Dickie Moore (*Little Men,* the *Our Gang* shorts, and *Heaven Can Wait*).

The *Our Gang* shorts involved George "Spanky" McFarland, Darla Hood, Carl "Alfalfa" Switzer, Billie "Buckwheat" Thomas, and Eugene "Porky" Lee. Dick worked with Alfalfa again when both were men in *Redwood Forest Trail.*

A child actor better-known for his behind screen work was Gene Reynolds, with whom Dick appeared in both *Babes in Toyland* and *Adventure in Washington.*

Classifying Frankie Darro as child or adult is difficult. He played teens, yet in the early years Dick shared a set with him, his roles almost always involved adult-level action. He played Bobby in *Burn 'Em Up Barnes*; Dan in *Little Men*; Jerry/Little Brave Heart in *The Great Adventures of Wild Bill Hickok*; the voice of Lampwick in *Pinocchio*; and Gig in *Sons of New Mexico.*

Sammy McKim and Dick were friends but didn't work together until *The Great Adventures of Wild Bill Hickok.* They both appeared in *Mister Smith Goes to Washington* and *The Adventures of Mark Twain* and competed for the role of the title character's voice in *Pinocchio.* Sammy was in *The Lone Ranger* serial for which Dick and Raymond Hatton filmed the bridges to merge it into the feature length film, *Hi-Yo Silver.*

Two young actresses worked with Dick twice, Ann [E.] Todd played his sister in both *Destry Rides Again* and *Brigham Young,* and Juanita Quigley played Helen McCoy as a child, the girl member of the gang in *Devil's Party,* and also Dick's little sister in *The Vanishing Virginian.*

Dick appeared in a couple of films with some big names in the business. Perhaps his favorite was Buck Jones, "The Cowboy Hero's Hero." *Smoke Tree Range* and *Hollywood Round-Up* both starred Buck and featured Dick.

Another favorite to work with was Errol Flynn, with whom he made *Rocky Mountain* and *Virginia City.*

Appendix II

Having experienced sufficient, "go away, kid, you bother me," Dick respected and admired James Stewart, who treated him like a person. They first met on *Wife vs. Secretary*, and also were together in *Destry Rides Again* and *Mister Smith Goes to Washington*.

Even though Dick worked twice with Humphrey Bogart, Bogie failed to leave a lasting memory. Dick played his son in *Black Legion* and was also in *Virginia City* with him.

Dick and Randolph Scott appeared in two films together, *Virginia City* and *Fort Worth*.

Another who left him without a memory was Ronald Reagan. They both performed in *Girls on Probation*, *Love Is on the Air*, and *Knute Rockne, All American*.

Someone Dick respected and who was seen in the same film as Dick twice, though they only worked together once, was Harry Carey, Sr. By the time Dick knew him, he was a character actor, but in early films, he was a hero. They were in *Sutter's Gold* and also *Mister Smith Goes to Washington*.

Dick liked Dick Foran and was featured as the child in one of Foran's early Westerns, *Moonlight on the Prairie*. He was also in *Land Beyond the Law* and *Black Legion* with Foran.

One of the B-Western heroes with whom Dick worked several times was Wild Bill Elliott. Dick enjoyed being on set with him. Together they were in *Moonlight on the Prairie* and *The Great Adventures of Wild Bill Hickok*. Elliott and Dick also were both in *Wonder Bar* and *Devil's Party*.

Another B-Western hero Dick enjoyed from *Wild Horse Round-up* on through his television years was Kermit Maynard. Kermit was the star of *Wild Horse Round-up*, and they were again together in *The Great Adventures of Wild Bill Hickok*, *Fort Worth*, and *Last of the Pony Riders* and into television episodes of *The Range Rider* and *Buffalo Bill, Jr.*

In his post-World War II years, Dick appeared in five films with cowboy hero Gene Autry. Those films were *Strawberry Roan*, *Sons of New Mexico*, *Wagon Team*, *The Old West*, and *Last of the Pony Riders*.

Fewer actresses made duplicate appearances with Dick. One who was "the girl" in two of Dick's early Westerns was Sheila Bromley, who was using the name Sheila Mannors at that time. She was in *Moonlight on the Prairie* and *Westward Ho* before changing her name and playing the bad girl in *Nancy Drew . . . Reporter* and *Girls on Probation*.

Also in *Girls on Probation* was Jane Bryan, who worked with Dick in *The Man Who Dared*.

Appearing twice with Dick were Erin O'Brien-Moore, who played his surrogate mother in *Little Men* and his mother in *Black Legion*; Evelyn Venable, who voiced the Blue Fairy in *Pinocchio* and played the pretty, young schoolteacher in *The Frontiersmen*; perky Spring Byington, Dick's mother in *The Vanishing Virginian* and aunt in *Heaven Can Wait*; and Anne Shirley, who grew up to be his sister in *A Man to Remember* and became his sister by marriage in *Stella Dallas*.

Hattie McDaniel was in three of Dick's films, *Little Men*, *The First Baby*, and *Maryland*, as was Gail Davis, who appeared in three of the Autry films, *Sons of New Mexico*, *Wagon Team* and *The Old West*. However, Davis went on to appear in a number of television episodes with Dick, spending more screen time in the long run.

The woman who shared the most big screen credits with Dick was Jane Darwell, whom he spoke of with a great deal of respect. She was in *Wonder Bar*, *The First Baby*, *Brigham Young,* and *Redwood Forest Trail*.

Character actor Robert Barrat had a role in the first film in which Dickie performed and shared billing with him several more times. He was in *Wonder Bar, Moonlight on the Prairie, Exclusive Story, Black Legion, Love Is on the Air,* and *The Adventures of Mark Twain*.

Some other character actors with whom Dick worked more than once were Henry Brandon, Barnaby in *Babes in Toyland,* Joe Dombrowski in *Black Legion* and the opera impresario in the *Our Gang Follies of 1938*; John Litel as Tommy Smith in *Black Legion*, Carson Drew in *Nancy Drew . . . Reporter*, Marshall in *Virginia City*, Committee Chairman in *Knute Rockne, All American* and Morgan Wheeler in *The Wild Dakotas*; and Herbert Rawlinson, Sir James Blake in *Blake of Scotland Yard*, George Copelin in *Love Is on the*

Air, Mr. Redmann in *The Kid Comes Back* and Senator Jenkins in *Adventure in Washington*.

Christian Rub gave voice to Gepetto in *Pinocchio* and had a role in *The Adventures of Mark Twain*, too. Willie Fung joined Litel and Dick in *Nancy Drew . . . Reporter* as the restaurant manager and also worked with Dick as Ling Wong in *Border Wolves* and took a part in *The Adventures of Mark Twain*.

Alan Hale, Sr. entertained Dickie royally with the pranks he and his friends played on each other on the set of *Virginia City*. He also had roles in *Stella Dallas* and *The Adventures of Mark Twain*. Pudgy, notable Billy Gilbert worked with Dick in the short *Who's Looney Now*. They were both also seen in *Sutter's Gold*, *The First Baby*, and *Destry Rides Again*.

Dick remembered Clarence Muse as a singer from *Daniel Boone*. He also appeared on the bill with Dick in *Kid Millions*, *Maryland* and *Heaven Can Wait*. Irving Bacon was in the cast of one of Dick's first year films, *Little Men*. His career continued into Dick's Autry years with *Sons of New Mexico*. Between those they were both in *Nancy Drew . . . Reporter* and *The Howards of Virginia*.

Old-timers J. Farrell MacDonald and Lafe McKee appeared in a few films with Dick, for MacDonald they include *Burn 'Em Up Barnes*, *Exclusive Story* and *Flying Fists* and for McKee, *Trail of the Hawk* and *Queen of the Jungle*. Horace B. Carpenter, who also went back to silents, was with Dick in *Burn 'Em Up Barnes*, *Flying Fists*, *The Great Adventures of Wild Bill Hickok* and *Mountain Rhythm*.

During Dick's screen years some fine actors specialized in villainous roles. Two of those Dick worked with more than once were Jason Robards, Sr. in *Burn 'Em Up Barnes*, *Sky Patrol* and *The Howards of Virginia* and Samuel S. Hinds, often a crooked judge, in *Black Legion*, *Devil's Party*, *Destry Rides Again* and *Adventure in Washington*. Another great villain was Laird Cregar who was in *This Gun for Hire* and *Heaven Can Wait*, though Dick shared no screen time with him.

Three of the greats who specialized in Western villains were in films with Dick, George Chesebro, Charles King, and John Merton. Chesebro threatened in *Queen of the Jungle*, *The Great Adventures of Wild Bill Hickok*, *Destry Rides Again* and *Virginia City*. King was in *Exclusive Story*, *Sutter's Gold* and *Smoke Tree Range*. Merton was a menace in *Daniel Boone*, *Wild Horse Round-Up*, *Land of Fighting Men* and *The Old West*.

Dick enjoyed working with both Guinn "Big Boy" Williams and Fuzzy Knight. He and Williams shared time in *Flying Fists*, *Virginia City* and *Rocky Mountain*, while Knight was in *Flying Fists*, *Brigham Young* and *Border Wolves*.

Also in *Flying Fists* was Herman Brix, better-known as Bruce Bennett. He was with Dick in *Blake of Scotland Yard* and *Land of Fighting Men*.

The hero in *Blake of Scotland Yard* was Ralph Byrd, who played Jerry Sheehan. He played Dick's screen father in *The Howards of Virginia*.

Interestingly, the director of *Blake of Scotland Yard*, *Queen of the Jungle* and *Flying Fists*, Robert F. Hill, also took a role in *Flying Fists*.

Taking roles in films in which Dick appeared were several stuntmen including Yakima Canutt. He was in *Westward Ho*, *Rocky Mountain*, and many more. In that time period, stunt players were not credited, so it is almost impossible to make an accurate record of who worked on what. Yak can be plainly seen in these as can Hank Bell in the opening sequence of *Westward Ho*.

Quite a few of the old pros Dick worked with during his childhood were still plying their trade when television burst into the living rooms of the nation. A number of them would appear in *The Range Rider* or *Buffalo Bill, Jr.* TV series along with Dick.

One actor who appeared in the first film Dick made shared the small screen with him in *Buffalo Bill, Jr.* Harry Woods, noted slick villain of the B-Westerns of the 1930s was in *Wonder Bar*, *Call of the Savage*, *Land Beyond the Law*, and *The Adventures of Mark Twain*, as well as television.

Starting association with Dick in the twelve chapter serial, *Burn 'Em Up Barnes* were Al Bridge, also in *The Adventures of Frank Merriwell*, *The Great Adventures of Wild Bill Hickok* and *Mister Smith Goes to Washington*; Stanley Blystone with *Devil's Party* and *Fort Worth*; and Julian Rivero in *Land Beyond* the Law, *The Great Adventures of Wild Bill Hickok*, *This Gun for Hire*, and *The Outlaw*.

Surprisingly, Raymond Hatton was in *Fifteen Wives* rather than a Western to start out, then *Exclusive Story*, *Hi-Yo, Silver*, *Love Is on the Air*, and, after the television work, *Requiem for a Gunfighter*. Stanley Andrews began in *Call of the Savage*. After that came *Sutter's Gold*, *The Lone Ranger* stock footage for *Hi-Yo Silver*, *Mister Smith Goes to Washington*, *Maryland*, and *Brigham Young*.

A John Wayne Western put Glenn Strange and Herman Hack with Dick. In addition to *Westward Ho*, Strange was also in *Moonlight on the Prairie*, *Land Beyond the Law*, and *Border Wolves*. Hack was uncredited in so many films and television episodes that it is difficult to gauge the volume of his credits. He was with Dick in *Westward Ho*, *Border Wolves*, *The Great Adventures of Wild Bill Hickok*, *Last of the Pony Riders*, and *The Old West*, and was still working later when Dick made *Requiem for a Gunfighter*.

Earle Hodgins worked in *Moonlight on the Prairie*, *Smoke Tree Range*, and *The Great Adventures of Wild Bill Hickok* before television with Dick. Noted stuntman, character actor and top-notch handler of horses, Bud Osborne also connected with Dick in *Moonlight on the Prairie*, followed by *The Adventures of Frank Merriwell*, *Sutter's Gold*, *Land Beyond the Law*, *Virginia City*, *The Adventures of Mark Twain*, and *Fort Worth*.

Ed Cobb was also in *The Adventures of Frank Merriwell*, as well as *Land Beyond the Law*, *Smoke Tree Range*, *The Great Adventures of Wild Bill Hickok* and *Mister Smith Goes to Washington*. He made an appearance in *Requiem for a Gunfighter*, too.

Classic villain Dick Curtis was in *Daniel Boone*, *Wild Horse Round-Up* (in which he got to play a good guy) and *Blake of Scotland Yard*. He masterminded some villainy in *The Range Rider* on television.

Lane Chandler and Dick were together in *Girls on Probation*, *Land of Fighting Men*, *The Howards of Virginia*, *Virginia City*, and *Requiem for a Gunfighter*. Chief Thundercloud, who played Geronimo in the first episode of *Buffalo Bill, Jr.*, was also in *Renfrew of the Royal Mounted* and *The Great Adventures of Wild Bill Hickok*.

Sam Flint, as Inspector Henderson, shared many scenes with Dickie in *Blake of Scotland Yard* and was also in *Mountain Rhythm* and *Strawberry Roan*. George DeNormand was also in *Blake of Scotland Yard* as well as in *Hollywood Round-Up*, *Devil's Party*, and *The Wild Dakotas*.

Tom London went back to silents, but didn't share the screen with Dick until *The Great Adventures of Wild Bill Hickok*. After that, he was in *Brigham Young* and *The Old West* before the television work. Steve Clark was also in *The Great Adventures of Wild Bill Hickok* as well as *Flying Fists*, *Hollywood Round-Up*, *Nancy Drew . . . Reporter*, and *Fort Worth*.

Bob Woodward was on screen much more as a double or a driver than with lines of his own in *Hollywood Round-Up*, *The Frontiersmen*, and *The Old West*, and did stunts in *Moonlight on the Prairie*. He held the same position when he and Dick moved to television.

George J. Lewis was a regular on the TV shows with Dick, but did manage to share credits in a couple of films, *Beware, Spooks!* and *Wagon Team*. House Peters, Jr. also spent more television time with Dick, but went back to an early film, appearing in *The Adventures of Frank Merriwell* and later *The Old West*. William "Bill" Henry also was in an earlier film, *A Man to Remember*, and in *The Wild Dakotas*, filmed in the same period as the *Buffalo Bill, Jr.* television series.

Not working with Dick until after World War II were a few who mainly appeared on the television shows. I. Stanford Jolley had been around a while, but did not share credits with Dick until *Sands of Iwo Jima* and later *The Wild Dakotas*. Sheb Wooley was one of the band in *Rocky Mountain* and also in *Fort Worth*. Gregg Barton, a fixture in Flying A television, appeared in *Fort Worth*, *Wagon Team* and *Last of the Pony Riders*. Don C. Harvey was also in *Fort Worth* and in *The Old West*. Robert "Buzz" Henry, a young rider like Dick and a stuntman, worked with him in *Rocky Mountain*. The friends also were on screen together in *Last of the Pony Riders* and *Bamboo Prison* and in the *Buffalo Bill, Jr.* episode, "Legacy of Jesse James."

Several actors and actresses were seen in *The Range Rider* and/or *Buffalo Bill, Jr.* television series, who had made only one film with Dick in his earlier years. Those included Francis McDonald in Dick's first foray into serials, *Burn 'Em Up Barnes*, Robert J. Wilkie—billed then as Bob—in *Woman Doctor*, Pamela Blake and Sarah Padden in *This Gun for Hire*, John Hamilton in *Adventure in Washington*, Walter Reed in *Angel on the Amazon*, Clayton Moore in *Sons of New Mexico*, and Fred Krone in *Last of the Pony Riders*. Rand Brooks, after working in *The Range Rider*, would appear in Dick's last credited film, *Requiem for a Gunfighter*.

Appendix III
Questionable Credits

THE FOLLOWING CREDITS are listed for Dick on Internet Movie Database but are erroneous or unproved. Dick said he did not do them. My comments are on the films I was able to locate and watch.

Washee Ironee (1934)
I've looked. He's not there.

The Pecos Kid (1935) Donald Pecos as a boy.
Nope. It's Dickie Moore.

Life Returns (1935) (uncredited) Newsboy.
Not seen film.

Silk Hat Kid (1935) (uncredited) Jimmy.
Not seen film.

O'Shaughnessy's Boy (1935) (uncredited) Boy with Sling Shot at Parade.
Not seen film.

Little Lord Fauntleroy (1936) (uncredited) Ceddie at age seven.
Nope. The child seen from the back only is not Dickie. Wrong head shape, wrong hair pattern, wrong voice, wrong body movement.

36 Hours to Kill (1936) (uncredited) Little Boy Selling *The Garden Beautiful*.
Not seen film.

Love Begins at Twenty (1936) (uncredited) Boy on Streetcar.
Not seen film.

Pepper (1936) (uncredited) Member of Pepper's Gang.
Not seen film.

The Man I Marry (1936) (uncredited) Little Boy.
Not seen film.

Ready, Willing and Able (1937) (uncredited) Junior.
Not seen film.

Love, Honor and Behave (1938) (uncredited) Boy Playing with Young Ted.
Not seen film.

On Borrowed Time (1939) Boy in tree.
I've looked. I can't find him in the tree or anywhere else in this film.

The Singing Dude (1940) Bud.
Not seen film.

Musical Movieland (short) (1944) (uncredited) Tourist.
Not seen film.

The Bridges at Toko-Ri (1954) (uncredited) Pilot.
Dick was old enough to know whether or not he was in this film. No.

Attila (1954)
Dick was old enough to know whether or not he was in this film. No.

Index of Film Titles

(Photos indicated with bold type.)

Adventure in Washington aka *Senate Pageboys* 107-108
Adventures of Frank Merriwell, The 18-19
Adventures of Mark Twain, The 7, 110-111
Along Came Jones 160
Babes in Toyland aka *March of the Wooden Soldiers* 7-8
Bambi 100
Black Legion 76
Blackboard Jungle, The 131
Blake of Scotland Yard 20-30, **21**, **22**, **24**, **25**, **26**, **28**, **29**
Border Wolves 58-60, 67
Boy and His Dog, A 144-146, **145**
Brigham Young 71-72, 93
Burn 'Em Up Barnes 12-13, **12**
Call of the Savage 15, 17-18, **17**

Cool and the Crazy, The 131-135, **132**, **133**
Daniel Boone 46-47
Destry Rides Again 71, 92-94
Devil's Bedroom, The 141-144, **142**, **144**, 152
Devil's Party 79, 109
Exclusive Story 74
Fifteen Wives xiv, 9, **10**
First Baby, The **74**, 75
Flying Fists 30, 76-79, **78**
Frontiersmen, The 60-63
Gasoloons 75
Girls on Probation 75-76
Great Adventures of Wild Bill Hickok, The 45, 63-67
Hawk, The aka *Trail of the Hawk* 37, 40-43
Heaven Can Wait 111-112
High School Confidential 131
Hi-Yo Silver 67-68
Hollywood Round-Up 54-58, **59**
Howards of Virginia, The 106-107
Iron Horse, The 46
Kid Comes Back, The 83-84, 159
Kid Millions 11-12, **11**
Land Beyond the Law 47
Land of Fighting Men **51**, 52
Last of the Pony Riders 120, 121
Life of Vergie Winters, The 9
Little Men 13
Little Women 13
Lone Ranger, The 67
Love Is on the Air 79
Major and the Minor, The 160
Man to Remember, A 84-86, **85**
Man Who Dared, The 84
March of the Wooden Soldiers aka *Babes in Toyland* 7-8
Maryland 105, 109-110
Mister Smith Goes to Washington 92, 94-95, 96, 107, 108
Moonlight on the Prairie 37, 44-46, 66
Mountain Rhythm 110
Nancy Drew . . . Reporter 86-89
Now and Forever 9
Old West, The 19
Our Gang Follies of 1936 32, **33**

Our Gang Follies of 1938 35-36, **36**
Outlaw, The 72
Pecos Kid, The xiv
Pigskin Palooka, The 8, 34-35, **35**, 36
Pinch Singer, The 33-34, 36
Pinocchio xiii, xiv, 13, 63, 97, 98-103, 152, 164
Queen of the Jungle 15-17, **16**
Redwood Forest Trail 120-121
Reefer Madness 131
Renfrew of the Royal Mounted 50-52
Requiem for a Gunfighter 137-140, **139**
Rocky Mountain 38, 123-130, 164
Sands of Iwo Jima 121-122
Senate Pageboys aka *Adventure in Washington* 107-108
Sergeant Madden 80
Shadow of a Boomerang 121
Sky Patrol 80-81
Smoke Tree Range 52-54, **53**
Snow White and the Seven Dwarfs 100
Sons of New Mexico 120
Stella Dallas 97, 98, 113, 114
Strange Wives 9, **10**
Strawberry Roan 52, 119, 120, 153-154, 164
Sutter's Gold 75
This Gun for Hire 52, 108
Trail of the Hawk aka *The Hawk* 37, 40-43
Vanishing Virginian, The 108-110, **109**
Virginia City 68-71
Westward Ho 37-38, **39**, 59, 67
Who's Looney Now 75
Wife vs. Secretary 91-92
Wild Dakotas, The 121
Wild Horse Round-Up 47-50
Woman Doctor 86
Wonder Bar 6-7, 152, 164
Young Mister Lincoln 86

Index

(Photos indicated with bold type.)

Adams, Ernie **51**, 63
Adams, Ted **53**
Adventures of Pinocchio, The (book) 98
Aldrich Family, The/Henry Aldrich 114-118, 164
Allen, Rex 120, 121
Allen, Valerie 141, **142**
Ameche, Don 111, 112
Andrews, Stanley 67
Angel, Heather 46
Arnold, Edward 94
Arthur, Jean 95

Ates, Roscoe 63
Aubrey, Jimmy 23
Auer, Misha 94
Autry, Gene 13, 119-120, 152, 164, 166
Bainter, Fay 105
Bakalyan, Dick **132, 133**
Baker, Bob 58, 59, 60
Baker, Silver Tip 63
Barclay, Joan 20, **21, 22, 24, 29**
Barrat, Robert 7, 111
Beckett, Scotty **109**
Beery, Noah, Jr. 17-18
Beery, Wallace 80
Bell, Hank 38, 59, 63, 67
Benedict, William "Billy" **78**, 79
Bennet, Spencer Gordon, 137
Bennett, Bruce aka Herman Brix 30, **51**, 76, **78**
Bennett, Constance 102
Benny, Jack 117-118
Berkeley, Busby 6
Betty Boop 98
Blanc, Mel 100
Blue, Monte 63
Bodrie, Joe 149
Bogart, Humphrey 68, 76
Boles, John 9, 97, 114
Bond, Ward 68
Bowman, Lee 84
Boyd, William **62**
Bradbury, Robert North 37
Brandon, Henry 35
Bridge, Al 63
Briggs, Don **19**
Briggs, Harlan 85
Brissac, Virginia 93
Brix, Herman aka Bruce Bennett 30, **51**, 76, **78**
Broken Arrow (television show) 141
Bromley, Sheila aka Sheila Mannors 45, 75
Brooks, Rand 137
Brown, Jackie 110
Brown, Joe E. 79
Brown, Johnny Mack 137, **139**, 139-140

Bruce, Virginia 107
Bryan, Jane 75
Bud Murray School of Dance 5
Buetel, Jack 72
Buffalo Bill, Jr. xiii, 19, 29, 46, 47, 80, 164
Bupp, Tommy 79
Burns, Bob 63
Buster, Budd 63
Buttram, Pat 120, 152
Byington, Spring 108, **109**
Byrd, Ralph 20, **29**, 30, 106, **107**
Cameron, Rod 137, 138, 140
Cantor, Eddie 11
Canutt, Yakima 38, **39**, 124, 126
Capra, Frank 94, 95
Carey, Harry, Jr. **xvi**
Carey, Harry, Sr. 95
Carey, Marilyn Fix **xvi**
Carlisle, Mary 79
Carpenter, Horace B. 63
Carradine, John 46
Cassidy, Hopalong 60-62, **62**
Catlett, Walter 100
Chandler, Lane **51**, 137
Chesebro, George 63
Cobb, Edmund 63, 137
Coburn, Charles 111
Collodi, Carlo 98
Coogan, Jackie 80
Cooper, Gary 9, 160
Courtney, Chuck 148
Cowboy Rambler Radio Show 3, 113
Cregar, Laird 111
Crenna, Richard 117
Curtis, Alan 80
Curtis, Dick 30, 49-50
Curtis, Jack 38, **39**
Darnell, Linda 72
Darro, Frankie 12, 13, 64, **65**, 120
Darwell, Jane 71-72, **74**
Del Rio, Dolores 7
DeNormand, George 30

Dietrich, Marlene 92, 93
Disney Legends Award 102, 152, 165
Disney, Roy E. 165
Disney, Walt 98, 100, 164
Dix, Rollo **41, 44**
Donald Duck 89
Donlevy, Brian 92
Donnell, Jeff 120-121
Dorr, Lester **57**
Douglas, Chet 138
Douglas, Gordon 8, 9, 35
Duncan, Kenne 63
Dwan, Allan 122
Dwire, Earl 63
Edwards, Cliff "Ukulele Ike" 99, 152
Eisner, Michael 165
Elliott, Gordon "Wild Bill" 45, 66-67, **66**
Elliott, John 54
Ellis, Bobby 117
Ellis, Edward 84, **85**
Ellison, Harlan 145
English, John 9
Erwin, Stuart 74
Evans, Dale 152, 157
Evans, Muriel 52, **53**, 54
Fadden, Tom 92, 93
Farrell, William 24
Fibber McGee and Molly 117-118
Flint, Sam 23, **28**, 29
Flory Dory Sixtet, The 32
Flying A Productions 120
Flynn, Errol 68, 70-71, 123, 124, **129**, 164
Fonda, Henry 86
Foran, Dick 44, 45, 46, 47, 76
Forbes, Scott 124
Ford, John 46, 86
Francis, Kay 7
Fuller, Robert 148
Fung, Willie 60
Gable, Clark 91
Gallaudet, John 79
Gibson, Edmund Richard "Hoot" 1, 3-4, 164

Golden Boot Award **151**, 152, 165
Goldsmith, Clifford 114, 117
Grant, Cary 15, 106
Granville, Bonita 86, **87, 88**
Granville, Charlotte 9
Grapewin, Charlie 84
Grauman's Chinese Theatre 151
Grayson, Kathryn 109
Hack, Herman 137
Hadden, Robert 134
Hadley, Reed 63
Hale, Alan, Sr., 68, 70-71
Harding, Ann 9
Hardy, Oliver 7
Harlow, Jean 91, 92
Hasso, Signe 111
Hathaway, Henry 9
Hatton, Raymond 67, 137
Hayden, Russell 62
Henry, Robert "Buzz/Buzzy" 44, 121, 125
Hill, Howard 125-126
Hodgins, Earle 63
Hollywood Stuntman's Hall of Fame 152, 165
Hollywood Walk of Fame 149-151, **150**, 165
Holt, Jack 120
Hood, Darla 32-35, **33**, 101-102
Hopkins, Miriam 68
Horn, Lillian 159
Howes, Reed 15, 17
Hughes, Chris 138
Hughes, Lloyd 21
"Indian War Party" 152
Inescort, Freida 86
Irwin, Boyd 80
Ives, Raymond 117
Jagger, Dean 72
Jason, Sybil 86
Johnson, Chubby 124
Johnson, Don **145**
Jolson, Al 6-7, 11, 164
Jones, Betty xvi, 4, 87, 129, 131, **165**
Jones, Buck 52, **53**, 54, **56, 57, 58, 59**

Jones, L.Q. aka Justus McQueen 141, 142, 143, 144, 145, 146
Jordan, Betty 40, **41**, **42**
Joslyn, Allyn 111, 112
Kate Smith Hour, The 114
Kelk, Jackie 115-116, **116**, 117
Kendall, Cy 47
Kennedy, Edgar 75
Knight, Fuzzy 59, 60, 76, 77
Kodak Theater 150
Kohler, Fred, Jr. xiv
Kornman, Mary 15, **16**, 17
Lackteen, Frank 137
Ladd, Alan 108
Lake, Veronica 108
Lamarr, Hedy 102
Lampwick 98-99
Lane, Lola 12
Lane, Yancey 40, **41**, **42**, **43**, **44**
Laurel & Hardy 7-8
Laurel, Stan 7
Lawrence, Marc 80
Lederman, Ross 46
Lee, Mary 86, **87**, **88**, 89
Lewis, George J. 79, 80
Lloyd, Betty aka Beth Marion 48, **50**
Lombard, Carole 9
London, Tom 63
Loy, Myrna 91
Lucky Strike Theatre 120
Lupton, John 141, 143, 152
Lux Radio Theatre 98, 113, 114
MacDonald, J. Farrell 77, **78**
MacLane, Barton 83
McCoy, Tim 137, 138, 140
McFarland, George "Spanky," 32-36, **35**, **36**
McGlynn, Frank, Jr. 37
McGowan, J.P. 63
McKee, Lafe 17, **41**, 42
McKim, Sammy 64, 98
McLaglen, Victor 79
McNally, Stephen 138
McQueen, Justus aka L.Q. Jones 141, 142, 143, 144, 145, 146

Magers, Boyd 79
Mahoney, Jocko aka Jock O'Mahoney 152, 164
Mannors, Sheila aka Sheila Bromley 45, 75
Mapes, Ted 63
March, Fredric 15, 110, 111
Marion, Beth aka Betty Lloyd 48, **50**
Marlowe, Scott 131
Marshall, George 93
Marshall, Herbert 107
Martel, Jeanne 76, **78**
M.A.S.H. (television show) 107
Maynard, Ken 47
Maynard, Kermit 47-48, **48, 49, 50**, 63
Mazurki, Mike 138
Melody Ranch 160
Memphis Film Festival xv, 52, 54
Merkel, Una 92
Merton, John 48, **51**
Metcalfe, Bradley 37
Miller, Walter **17**
Mitchell, Robert and his St. Brendan's Boys aka The Robert Mitchell Boy Choir 62
Mix, Art 63
Mix, Tom 2
Montgomery, Jack 60, 63
Moore, Alvy 141, 142, 145
Moore, Constance 59
Moore, Dickie xiv, 13, 111, 112
Moorhead, Natalie **10**
Morgan, Frank 108, **109**
Morgan, Ralph 13
Morris, Wayne 83
Motion Picture and Television Hospital 52
Mulhall, Jack 12-13, **12**
Murray, Zon 137
Muse, Clarence 46, 47
Nash, Clarence 89
New York Times, The xiii
O'Brien, George 46
O'Brien-Moore, Erin 13, 76
O'Mahoney, Jock aka Jocko Mahoney 152, 164
O'Neil, Barbara 97, 114
Orlando, Don 42, **44**

Orpheum Theater 33
Ortego, Artie 63
Our Gang 5, 7, 8, 31, 36, 101, 112
Payne, John 15, 105
Perreau, Gigi 132
Perrin, Jack 63
Peters, House, Jr. 19
Petrie, Howard 123
Phelps, Buster **10**
Pickens, Slim 125
Powell, Dick 7
Powell, Lee 67
Power, Tyrone 72
Preston, Robert 108
Quigley, Juanita **109**
Rains, Claude 94, 95
Randall, Jack **51**, 52
Range Rider, The xiii, 19, 29-30, 46, 47, 67, 80, 152, 164
Rawlinson, Herbert 20, **28**, **29**, 30
Reagan, Ronald 79
Redwing, Rodd 152
Reed, Donald 50
Reynolds, Gene 107
Roach, Hal 7
Rockwell, Jack 63
Rogers, Ginger 160
Rogers, Jean 18
Rogers, Roy 152, 155, 157-158
Rooney, Mickey xiv
Rosen, Marvyn J. 132
Rosenbloom, Slapsie Maxie 83-84
Rub, Christian 100
Schaefer, Armand 12
Scott, Randolph 68, 71
Screen Actors Guild 93, 122
Shirley, Anne 86
Silver Spur Award 152, **153**
Spinner, Marilyn 15
Spot 124, 126-128, **127**, 130
Stanwyck, Barbara 97, 98, 114
Starrett, Charles 152
Steele, Bob 137, 138, 152

Steele, Tom 137
Steiner, Max 123
Sterler, Hermine 108
Stewart, James 91, 92, 93-94
Stone, Ezra 114, 117
Stone, George E. 45
Stone, Milburn 80
Sturgess, Olive 138
Switzer, Carl "Alfalfa," 32-36, **33**, **35**, **36**, 120-121
Taliaferro, Hal aka Wally Wales 63
Tearle, Conway **10**
Temple, Shirley xiv, 5, 9
Thomas, Billie "Buckwheat" **33**
Thomas, Frankie, Jr. 86, **87**, **88**, 89
Thundercloud, Chief 50, 63, 67
Todd, Ann (E.) 72, 93
Tokar, Norman 117
Travis, June 83
Trent, John 80
Tucker, Forrest **106**
Twelvetrees, Helen 54, 57, **59**
"Two-Fisted Justice" 30
Vallee, Rudy 114
Van Sickle, Dale 137
Venable, Evelyn 61, **62**, 63, 100
Wales, Wally aka Hal Taliaferro 63
Waller, Eddy 63
Ward, Blackjack 63
Ward, Russell 120
Wayne, Carole **64**
Wayne, Frank 23
Wayne, John 37, 59
Weaver Brothers 110
Weaver, Elviry 110
Western Clippings 148
"Western Edition" 30
Western, Johnny 148
Whitaker, Slim 63
Williams, Bill 121
Williams, Guinn "Big Boy" 68, 70-71, 76, 77, 125
Winninger, Charles 92
Withers, Grant 54

Witney, William 134, 135
Woodward, Bob 46, 54
Wyatt, Al 152
Wymore, Patrice 124
Yates, Herbert 122
Yellowjacket Boat Company 155

www.ingramcontent.com/pod-product-compliance
Lightning Source LLC
Chambersburg PA
CBHW071433150426
43191CB00008B/1115